Play With Your Dog

PAT MILLER

CPDT, CDBC

Publishing

Wenatchee, Washington U.S.A.

Play With Your Dog.
Pat Miller

Dogwise Publishing
A Division of Direct Book Service, Inc.
403 S Mission St.
Wenatchee, Washington 98801
1-800-776-2665
www.dogwisepublishing.com / info@dogwisepublishing.com

© 2008 Pat Miller

Cover Photo: Louis B. Ruediger
Cover Dog: Ruby, owned by Jane Killion
Indexing by: Cheryl Smith

Library of Congress Cataloging-in-Publication Data
Miller, Pat, 1951 Oct. 14-
   Play with your dog / by Pat Miller.
      p. cm.
   ISBN 978-1-929242-55-9
   1. Dogs--Behavior. 2. Play behavior in animals. 3. Games for dogs. I. Title.
   SF433.M57 2008
   636.7'0887--dc22
                                          2008018390

ISBN: 978-1-929242-55-9
Printed in the U.S.A.

DEDICATION

To Paul, my wonderful husband, playmate and life partner,
who, I confess, is really much better at playing with dogs
than I am; and to Tucker, exceptional canine playmate and
beloved family member, forever in our hearts.

*Tucker, our Australian Cattle Dog mix, was adopted from
the Marin Humane Society when he was nine weeks old. He
was Paul's close companion and favorite playmate throughout
his life. The two of them were the epitome of canine-human
play partners. Tucker succumbed to prostate cancer in May of
2007, at age 14.*

Contents

INTRODUCTION

We've all seen those dogs whose philosophy of life seems to be "You can never have too much fun!" Indeed, watch a litter of puppies at play and you're instantly convinced that having fun is a natural, hardwired behavior for dogs. No one has to train puppies to play—they just do it. So why do some adult dogs not play well, or even not seem to know how to play at all?

When I do behavior assessments of shelter dogs, I frequently encounter dogs who don't know how to play. I offer all different kinds of play opportunities, and they look at me with a confused or blank stare, or worse, they appear frightened of my attempts to engage them in a friendly frolic. Sadly, despite the fact that playing with other puppies is a hardwired social behavior, and given that some may just be too stressed to play at the moment, many of these dogs never learned how to play with humans—a related but somewhat different behavior, but one that is not genetically programmed into little puppy brains.

Some adult dogs also lose the natural-born knack of playing with other dogs. This can be due to a lack of early and ongoing socialization with other dogs. However, some dogs, as they mature, simply aren't interested in playing with every Spot, Jock, and Harry that comes along. Although dogs are a social species, that doesn't mean they get along with every conspecific (a member of the same species) on the planet. After all, we humans are a social species, and we sure don't all get along!

Many dog owners are more interested in having a canine companion who can lie quietly on the rug than they are a dog who can catch a Frisbee™ in mid-air or romp through an agility course. So where's the harm if a dog doesn't know how to play? The harm is that one of the inarguable benefits of play is that it builds relationships. Dogs who don't play with their owners may be at significantly greater risk of being rehomed, or even euthanized, if the relationship fails.

It's no coincidence, I firmly believe, that so many shelter dogs are mystified at the concept of human-play. A dog ends up at an animal shelter or rescue group because the social contract—the one that says the dog deserves a lifelong loving home—has been broken, usually by his human. Often, the same humans who can't be bothered to play with their dogs are the ones who don't understand, or appreciate, the relationship component of dog-husbandry.

"Moving, can't keep," is one of reasons most commonly listed for owner surrender on a shelter dog's paperwork. It's true that one must make an extra effort and commitment to take the family dog along when relocating—whether across the country or around the block. But, I dare say, millions of dog owners do just that when they move, however much it complicates the moving arrangements. These caring and responsible canine guardians wouldn't dream of giving up their beloved companions just because they're moving. So what makes the difference between "Moving, can't keep" and the owner who would live in his car before he'd abandon his best friend?

In one word: relationship. The dog-human social contract is all about our relationship with our dogs. Play builds relationships—hence the importance of play. As kids, we make new friends by playing with them. The ones with whom we form lifelong relationships are likely to be the ones with whom we spend the most time and have the most fun sharing mutually rewarding and enjoyable activities.

Play. All dogs need to play. The style of play will vary, but all dogs will be mentally and physically more healthy if they play. In addition to helping build a solid relationship between you and your dog, playing with your canine friend will:

- Help your dog develop and retain valuable social skills

- Provide superb mental and physical exercise

- Offer excellent training opportunities

- Add valuable and varied reinforcers to your training toolbox

- Assist with behavior modification programs

Whether you and your dog already play together and are looking for more creative opportunities to play, or you have a play-deprived dog who needs a re-introduction to the joys of play, this book should help you pour even more mortar into the foundation of your relationship with your well-loved canine companion. Don't spend too much time reading, though—be sure to save time for play!

Chapter 1
THE PLAY'S THE THING
WHAT IS PLAY?

Watching puppies play is inarguably one of the most delightful and amusing pastimes on earth. Still, there are reasons for puppy-play that are far more compelling than simply making dog owners and the dog gods chuckle. The role of play in a canid's development has been well-studied by ethologists (someone who studies animal behavior, especially as it occurs in its natural environment). But what, exactly, is play?

One response might be, "Like pornography, I may not be able to define it, but I know it when I see it." Surprisingly, however, some people (both dog owners and non-dog owners) are frighteningly poor at identifying dog play. Some perceive perfectly appropriate "dog play" as dangerous, while others are oblivious to the risks they're taking by allowing their dogs to engage in play that encourages and reinforces inappropriate behaviors.

When it came time for the first night of after-class play-time in a recent Good Manners class of mine, the owner of an adolescent Poodle mix was clearly quite distressed. She was extremely reluctant to allow Luna to play. Her dog, she told us, was quite aggressive toward other dogs. She'd

Watching puppies play is one of the most delightful and amusing pastimes on earth.

tried allowing her to play with friends' dogs, but had always stopped the play immediately because her dog was biting. I was surprised at her comments, as Luna had done quite well in class and not demonstrated any behavior that raised any red flags for me.

I'm not one to lightly discount an owner's observations or concerns about her dog's behavior. However, I convinced Luna's owner to let her dog play with one other dog in a very controlled environment.

As we watched, the dogs began a session of perfectly normal play, including some mouthing and play-growling. The owner's face paled, and in a panic she exclaimed, "See? See? That's what I mean!"

I quickly reassured her that the dogs were play biting and growling, and that there was no cause for alarm. Somewhat dubious, she agreed to allow the play to continue. Over time, she realized that her beloved dog's behavior was perfectly normal and acceptable, and was thrilled that Luna could play well with others.

Play can look almost like "real" serious behavior.

In a case of failure to recognize inappropriate play behavior, a family came to see me for a private consult with their 2-year-old Jack Russell Terrier. The dog had recently bitten their 11-year-old son's face, inflicting a wound that required five sutures. Since the time Scooter was a puppy, the family's two children, then 5 and 9, now 7 and 11, were allowed to play roughly with the dog: pulling his legs; running away and screaming when the pup chased after them biting at their heels; tossing a blanket over him and roughing him up through the blanket; grabbing his ball away from him; and hugging and kissing the little dog, even when Scooter snarled a protest. It was the hug and kiss that had elicited the bite to the boy's lip, after the boy ignored the warning snarl and kissed the dog again.

Since at least some of us humans seem to be not-so-good at correctly identifying play, let's see how some ethologists define it. Gordon Burghardt, Ph.D., at the University of Tennessee in Knoxville, offers the following 5-point definition of play:

1. Performance of the behavior is not completely functional in the context in which it is expressed.

2. Play behavior is spontaneous, voluntary, intentional, pleasurable, rewarding, or done for its own sake (only one of these need apply).

3. Play differs from "serious" performance of a behavior in at least one respect—it is incomplete, exaggerated, awkward, precocious, or involves behavior patterns with modified form, sequencing, or targeting.

4. Behavior is performed repeatedly, in similar, but not rigidly, stereotyped form.

5. Play is initiated when animals are adequately fed, healthy, and free from stress—they are in a "relaxed field." Play is one of the first behaviors to cease when animals are hungry, threatened, or under environmental stress.

In plain English, the above definition of play might look like this:

1. Play doesn't have to have a function or make sense, other than to have fun.

2. Play is fun, it's done on purpose, and/or it feels good.

3. Play can look almost like "real" serious behavior—but not quite (hence Luna's owner's confusion).

4. Play behavior is repeated in patterns, but not rigid ones.

5. Animals don't play when they are sick, exceedingly hungry, or stressed.

The Social/Developmental Importance of Play

There is clear evidence that play is an important part of a puppy's social development. Ethologist and well-known author Mark Bekoff suggests that play is the means by which dogs learn appropriate restraint and inhibition over aggression and other socially inappropriate behaviors. In his study comparing the behavior of coyotes, dogs, and wolves, he found that the amount of play behavior a puppy exhibited (versus aggressive behavior) was a reliable indicator of how social the animal was as an adult. That is, puppies who play are likely to be friendlier and more socially well-adjusted as adults. Because social status is more fluid during play, higher ranking pups have the opportunity to learn the value of cooperation and submission (other pups are more willing to keep playing with them), increasing the probability that they will also choose to use those strategies in other, non-play social interactions.

Although there is a marked lack of scientific studies on the subject, a wealth of anecdotal evidence from trainers and behavior professionals indicates a significant impact on the development and behavior of orphaned pups as well as those weaned or taken away from litters too early. Resulting undesirable behaviors can include lack of bite inhibition; reactivity; anxiety; aggression or fearfulness with other dogs; and an inability to present, interpret, and/or respond appropriately to canine body language.

Play and the Human/Animal Bond

While Bekoff studied behavior among conspecifics, there is clearly a similar social benefit resulting from play between dogs and their humans. One of the reasons dogs hold their lofty position as Man's (and Woman's) Best Friend, is that they share our joy of playing. While most species romp and play as juveniles, dogs and humans are among the few who continue to play enthusiastically into old age. And while the best trainers are masters at incorporating play into training to keep the process exciting and enjoyable, the best play may be that which is done purely for its own sake,

One of the reasons dogs hold their position as (wo)man's best friend is that they share our joy of playing.

where thoughts and cares of the world are set aside, and you and your dog just share a rousing game of tag, chase, or fetch just for the sheer, mindless fun of it.

The advantages that Bekoff noted for conspecific play are significant to dog-human play as well. Dogs who learn how to play well with humans are also likely to be more social with people and more able to cooperate and defer when interacting with them.

There is no shortage of support for dog-play from the dog behavior community:

- Dog behavior consultant Steven R. Lindsay reminds us, "Where there is no play, there is no relationship or meaning." People who play sincerely with their dogs can't help but develop a connection with them.

- Stanley Coren, professor of psychology at the University of British Columbia and author of a number of books on dog behavior, says it so well in his book *How to Speak Dog*, "To watch dogs run in play is to appreciate grace and joy. It is also a key to understanding something about their psychology: Running is to dogs what dancing is to people. It is their way to get into the rhythm of the Universe."

- In her fantastic book on dog-human relationship, *The Other End of the Leash*, animal behaviorist Patricia McConnell says, "Play is good for our spirits, our bodies and our minds. It teaches us, both dogs and humans, to coordinate our efforts with others, to learn to inhibit ourselves even when excited, and to share the ball even when we want it for ourselves."

• Paul Owens, acclaimed non-violent dog trainer from Southern California, lists "play" as the second of "The Nine Ingredients for Optimum Health and Growth" in his excellent book, *The Dog Whisperer* (which predates the television dog personality of the same designation by several years), and reminds us that play keeps life interesting, unpredictable and exciting, and prevents dogs—and humans—from succumbing to boredom-related undesirable behaviors.

Dogs and children seem to share an innate and unbridled joy of play—which is why an adult who suffers from being too serious about life may be told to find her "Inner Child." Jeffrey Moussaieff Masson talks about dogs and children playing in *Dogs Never Lie About Love*:

> Dogs chase twigs and leaves and their own tails and drops of water and butterflies; they leap in the air and burrow in the sand, dig holes, and throw themselves into waves. What child does not engage in such behavior as well? Perhaps this is why children and puppies can play together for hours on end in a garden or on the beach. They play in almost exactly the same way.

Dogs who learn to play with littermates, and a bit later with their humans, never seem to lose their enjoyment of play. We humans, if we're not careful, can forget about the importance of having fun. We may fall into the trap of allowing others to do our playing for us—watching little figures on the big screen in our living rooms play with footballs, baseballs, basketballs, and soccer balls, while our dogs gaze longingly up at us from the floor at our feet, hoping we'll take a break and play ball with them.

"Dogs chase twigs and leaves...and burrow in the sand, dig holes, and throw themsevles into waves."

It's not so hard. A workaholic myself, I sometimes need my dogs to remind me to play. Anytime I get up from my computer, Lucy, our Cardigan Corgi, leaps up and heads for the back door, her eyes bright with anticipation. Maybe it's time for a tongue-dragging session of Frisbee™. If I move to the front door she's right there as well—it might mean a trip to the barn, where she gets to chase her Genius™ toy up and down the aisle. If I start upstairs instead, she's right behind me, eager for a round of Patty-Paws on the bed. Even the dullest human couldn't mistake the "Let's play!" messages she sends, and no matter how busy I am, how pressing the next deadline, how rushed to meet with a client, it's almost impossible to resist at least a brief time-out from my schedule to accommodate her invitation. So we play.

The Language of Play: Reading Dogs

Dogs are masters at communicating through body language. Humans, not so much. Although we certainly rely on non-verbal communication in our relationships with each other, most members of our species haven't done a very good job of learning the language of dogs. Dogs, on the other hand, are quite good at reading ours, since their ability to get good stuff and avoid bad stuff depends on their ability to understand us.

They are also, for the most part, darned good at understanding each other, providing they've been given the opportunity to develop their social skills. If you study dogs playing and pay careful note to the ebb and flow of behavior as it relates to the signals they give each other, you'll learn a lot about canine communication. Most of the signals they use in play are also used in less frivolous interactions, but because dogs are aware of the play context, behaviors like a bite to the neck—a sure trigger for a fight in tenser times—are laughed off by playmates.

It's this ambiguousness that can give heart palpitations to concerned owners as they watch their beloved fur-babies romp with mock ferocity. Just remember that it's all about context. If two—or several—dogs are playing and it sounds or looks like not-fun to you, check out the participants more closely. If they all look like they're enjoying themselves and coming back for more, you can probably relax. If anyone is consistently trying to hide or escape or otherwise looks traumatized, then it's time for an intervention. Brief scuffles can even occur and it's still acceptable play—just one dog asking another in no uncertain terms to back off. But if a real fight goes down and doesn't resolve itself quickly (within a few seconds), then it's superhero time—someone needs rescuing. BE CAREFUL! One of the best ways to get bitten is trying to break up a dogfight. Be sure to read Chapter 2 for tips on breaking up a fight with as little risk to your own person as possible.

On a more positive note, here are some of the canine communication signals you're likely to see when dogs are playing:

- **Barking**. There is a wide variety of different barks dogs use to express themselves in different situations. The play-bark usually lacks the tone of intensity that's present when a dog is alarm barking or threat barking. Some dogs bark in the excitement of play, others bark as cheerleaders or "fun police" when two or more other dogs are engaged in play. Herding dogs often assume the cheerleader or fun police role.

- **Biting**. Dogs frequently bite in play. This behavior can confuse and worry novice dog owners, especially when it's combined with other mock-aggressive behaviors such as play-growling, snarling, barking, and snapping.

Dogs frequently bite in play.

A status-related appeasement or avoidance behavior when offered in a non-play encounter, this posture can be offered freely as a part of play.

- **Belly-Up**. A status-related appeasement behavior when offered in a non-play encounter, this posture can be offered freely as part of play, and dogs will often take turns being "the one on top"—a clear indication that it's being used in play and not as a serious statement about status.

- **Body-Slamming**. Some dogs love rough physical contact as part of play, and will run full-speed into their playmates.

- **Bounce**. Often occurs immediately following the play bow. The dog springs up from the bow toward his playmate to trigger a movement response from the other dog.

- **Chase**. Some dogs prefer non-contact sports, and will engage in full-speed chase-me rituals.

Some dogs prefer non-contact sports, and will engage in full-speed chase-me rituals.

- **Chew-face.** Teeth bared, mouths open, dogs are often lying down and biting energetically at each others' faces. You may hear lots of teeth clacking and mock growling.

- **Chin over shoulders.** Although this is a strong statement of status when not used in play, when used between play pals, it's just part of the sport of body contact. You will often see dogs in play happily take turns offering this behavior, which clearly makes it not about status.

- **Growling.** This is an important and valuable warning signal when given outside play, and is a mock warning in play; often offered when dogs are playing tug or "chew-face."

Although this is a strong statement of status when not used in play, between play pals it's just part of the sport.

- **Happy grin**. Corners of lips (commissure) are pulled back and relaxed, mouth is open and teeth and tongue are exposed. Can be an expression of fear when not used in play if dog is tense, or happiness/contentment if dog is relaxed.

- **Heel-biting**. Very common with herding breeds, who have been purposely selected for this trait as part of their herding repertoire.

- **Piloerection**. Often associated with aggression, a dog's hair can be raised on the back of his neck, his shoulders, and/or all the way down to and beyond the base of his tail. It's simply a sign of arousal, and can be play-arousal, or a sign of fear or aggression in a different context.

Don't take seriously whatever behavior follows the play-bow.

- **Play-bow**. Dog lowers front end while keeping hind end elevated. The very significant meaning of this behavior is "Don't take seriously whatever behavior follows." One dog can use the play-bow to invite another to play, and to let his playmate know that if he bites, growls, chases, or knocks the other dog off her feet, it's all just good clean fun. It may also be offered during play as an appeasement gesture, meaning "Oops, sorry, didn't mean to bite that hard!"

- **Play-down**. Alternative version of the play-bow, but dog drops all the way to the ground rather than keeping hindquarters elevated.

- **Stiffly wagging tail**. A sign of arousal and potential aggression in a non-play situation, this is also an expression of the dog's excitement when playing.

- **Whale eye/Wild eye/Eyes wide open.** There is no mistaking this expression of glee in a dog who is full of fun and play. The whites of the eyes are showing, often in conjunction with lowered shoulders and elevated chin. When not in play, this expression can be a strong indication of fear and/or pending aggression.

- **Zoomies/Puppy-Rushes/Frapping.** A delightful behavior that can be alarming to novice dog owners, and one that is not limited to puppies—this behavior appears to be an expression of pure glee and excess energy, as a dog tucks tail, lowers hindquarters, opens eyes wide, and zooms full speed around whatever space is available. The terms "zoomies" and "puppy rush" are self-explanatory; "frap" stands for "FRenetic Activity Period."

The best way to increase your understanding of your dog's language of play is to watch lots of dogs playing. Check out area dog parks, or see if your local doggie daycare centers will let you watch their canine clients in action, or on video cam. Set up play dates for your own dog with compatible canines.

When possible, video dog-play interactions yourself so you can study them later in your own living room, complete with instant replay, until you're very comfortable with your understanding of how dogs communicate in play. Watch for the subtleties of their signals—how one dog invites another and successfully engages her, how you know when play partners are both having a good time, how one dog tells another he's playing too rough, and how to tell that it's time to end a play session because one or more dogs aren't enjoying themselves. This will be useful to you when you're monitoring dog play to keep it appropriate, when you're trying to encourage a reluctant dog to play with you, or when you're looking for new ways to get your own dog to engage in play.

CHAPTER 2
PLAYS WELL
WITH OTHERS
CANINE PLAY STYLES

Dogs are social creatures—no one can argue with that. So are humans. We know that all humans don't get along with all humans—just check the nightly police blotter in any American town or city, or watch the evening news for an update on the latest international conflict if you need convincing. Still, for some reason many people expect that all dogs should get along with all dogs. They don't.

Dogs Playing With Dogs

In the wild, a canine social group is a closed society. Dogs from one wild pack don't invite the neighboring pack over for a spot of afternoon tea or a few innings of softball. Rather, if a dog wanders into a neighboring pack's territory, the potential for bloodshed is high, especially if the intruder ignores the home pack's clear warnings to leave. While we have purposely selected for more canine tolerance of "outsider" dogs over many thousands of years of domestication, it's still a very unreasonable expectation that all dogs should be able to get along with all dogs. Fortunately some dogs get along with most others, and *most* dogs get along with *some* others. There are a number of reasons for this.

We have enhanced the dog-social behavior of some breeds more than others by breeding for certain traits. The scent hounds—Beagles, Bassets, Foxhounds, etc., are much more likely to get along in groups due to selective breeding than the pugnacious terriers like Scotties, Jack Russells (Parsons Russells), and American Pit Bull Terriers. Sporting breeds such as Labrador and Golden Retrievers tend to be gregarious, while the working breeds—Akitas, Rottweilers, Great Danes—not so much. These are sweeping generalizations, of course; there are Beagles and Bassets who will fight with other dogs at the drop of a hat, and Pit Bulls who are the life of the dog park party.

In addition to genetics (nature), early socialization (nurture) plays a significant role in whether a dog will be dog-friendly as an adult. The all-critical socialization period from 4 weeks to 16 weeks is the time when a puppy learns what's good and safe in the world. Lack of early exposure to other dogs or traumatic early experiences with other dogs can convince a pup that playing with other canines is the last thing on earth he wants to do. If you want to maximize your dog's potential for playing well with others, be sure he has lots of opportunities to have *enjoyable* experiences with *appropriate* canine playmates during the first four months of his life—and beyond.

In between the dogs who are total party animals and those who are the canine equivalent of hermits, preferring to live in caves, are the majority of dogs—those who are selective about the other dogs with whom they choose to play. The choice is often based on several factors, including size, familiarity, sometimes breed recognition, and often, in large part, on play style.

Beagles are among the breeds more likely to get along in groups.

Scottish Terriers are not.

Canine Play Styles

Your best option for finding compatible playmates for your dog is to identify your dog's play style and select dogs of similar size, energy level, and play style preference.

Size matters. No doubt there are dogs of significant size disparity who can play well together, but as a general rule, it's wise to keep the difference in the realm of 25 pounds or less. A playful large dog can easily injure a little dog, even without intent to do harm, simply by running over or jumping on the smaller dog. Of even greater concern is a phenomenon known as predatory drift in which something from a dog's evolutionary past triggers the larger dog's brain to perceive the smaller dog as a prey object—a bunny or squirrel—instead of the canine pal he's played happily with for months, or years. Often the trigger is the smaller dog running, yelping, or squealing. The bigger dog gives chase, and tragedy ensues.

To avoid this, good dog parks offer—and enforce—separate play areas for smaller dogs, and wise owners of small dogs don't allow them to romp with canines who are considerably larger. Owners of big dogs sometimes mock owners of toy breeds for their "overprotectiveness," but the risk is very real. There are plenty of examples of small dogs, especially tough small dogs (Jack Russells come to mind) who routinely hold their own with larger playmates, and lots of tiny dogs live long and happy lives with much larger dogs. My own 8-pound Pomeranian shared his life unscathed with dogs in our family as much as ten times his size—although Dusty didn't really play with his large siblings; it was more like a peaceful coexistence. If you're actively looking for playmates for your dog, however, it's safest to keep size cautions in mind, as well as play styles.

Significant size disparity between playmates can lead to serious—sometimes fatal—complications. These two should be closely supervised, if allowed to play together.

If you know your dog's preferred play style, you can narrow his playmate pool to potentially suitable dogs without even attempting risky introductions. Here are common canine play styles:

- **Cheerleaders**. These dogs like to play on the fringes around other dogs who are actively engaged with each other (see Body Slammers, Chasers and Wrestlers). They are often from the herding group (Collies, Shepherds, etc.) and are usually quite vocal, often engaging in non-stop barking. Cheerleading is related to behaviors that have been enhanced for herding—herding dogs tend to be "control freaks." They may also nip at heels, and at the assertive "fun-police" end of the cheerleader behavior continuum, will actually try to break up the fun. If they do this with dogs who take offense, there is potential for dogfights. Playmates for cheerleaders need to be tolerant of these dogs' sometimes irritating efforts to control play activities.

- **Body Slammers**. These are the demolition derby dogs of the canine playground. Labs and Boxers are prominent in this group, although there are plenty of others for whom "play" means "run full speed into other dogs and see if you can knock them off their feet." Body Slammers play best with other Body Slammers, but can also be compatible with some Wrestlers and Chasers. They don't generally do well with Cheerleaders and Soft Touches. There is risk of minor to major bodily damage when big dogs run into each other at full speed. Think "T-bone" collision. A lot of the breeds who fall into the Body Slammer category seem to suffer from a higher-than-average incidence of ruptured ACLs. Hmmmmmmmmm.

- **Wrestlers**. Wrestlers are into full, prolonged body contact. These dogs are most likely to take turns being on top, and also tend to engage in rousing games of chew-face. This is a comparatively low-risk play-style, as long as both dogs are happy Wrestlers. If one dog insists on pinning another who isn't comfortable there, however, it can turn ugly. Watch your Wrestlers to be sure both are having a good time, and be prepared to intervene if you see emotions rising. A time-out is a good strategy if arousal levels are getting high—it gives both participants time to chill out and brings arousal levels back down.

Cheerleaders and "fun police" like to play on the fringes around other dogs who are actively engaged.

Body Slammers are the demolition derby dogs of the canine playground.

Wrestlers are into full, prolonged body contact.

- **Chasers**. These dogs just love to run. It's great fun to watch dogs play "catch me if you can." Some show a strong preference for the specific role of chaser or chasee, others are happily willing to take turns. This is one play-style where predatory drift is more likely to occur, so it's wise to keep your play pals similar in size for this game. A variation of Chase is Keep Away, where the chasee grabs a toy and invites the other dog to chase after her and try to get the toy. Keep Away often morphs into a mutually enjoyable game of tug.

- **Tuggers**. Just like it sounds, these are dogs who love to play tug, and are happy to do it with a canine playmate. Dog-tug is a fine game—just watch for resource guarding that can turn tug into war.

Chasers sometimes like to play Keep Away, where the chasee grabs a toy and invites the other dog to chase after her to try to get the toy.

Tucker and Lucy, two of our dogs, enjoy a game of dog-tug.

Here are two dogs who could entertain themsevles quite nicely with Self-Play.

- **Soft Touches**. Some dogs are very tentative about play. These may be dogs who were not well socialized and aren't yet sure how to interact confidently with other dogs, they may be dogs who have been injured or are arthritic and it hurts them to play hard, or they may just be dogs who don't like to roughhouse. Soft Touches should definitely play with other Soft Touches—they're too likely to find any other kind of play too mentally traumatic or physically painful.

- **Self-Play**. It always makes me chuckle to watch a dog engaged in self-play. This is the dog who tosses a toy in the air for herself, catches it, and tosses it again. I know some creative Border Collies who learned to carry a ball to the top of the stairs and push it off so they could run down and catch it, carry it upstairs and do it again. When she was alive, my wonderful Terrier mix, Josie, could entertain herself by rolling onto her back with a chew-toy in her mouth, lift the toy by grasping it with both front paws, hold it in the air and study it for a while, lower it back to her mouth and chew some more, then lift it and study it again, all while staying on her back. Like children, there's a certain joy in having a dog who can keep herself entertained!

Introducing Dogs

Okay, you've evaluated your dog's play style and found a potential playmate you think will be compatible. What now? Time for introductions.

Various training and behavior professionals offer different protocols for introducing new dogs to each other, but they almost universally agree that it's best done in neutral territory, where neither dog has home field advantage. If that's not possible, outdoors in one of the dog's safely-fenced yards is preferable to inside either of the dog's homes.

I introduce new dogs by letting them see each other at first, on-leash, at a distance of 20 to 50 feet, watching body language so the dogs can tell me how comfortable they are with each other. Ideally, you'll see calm, controlled interest—ears up and forward, but not pricked hard forward; tails waving at half-mast, not up and still or wagging stiffly; dogs making soft eye contact, not holding an extended hard stare.

Obviously, if you see barking, lunging, and snarling it's not a good match, and playtime is called off. Most likely you'll see something in between casual interest and outright aggression—an excited interest that's hard to read clearly. At this point I have handlers feed their dogs bits of very high value treats to give the dogs a good association with each other's presence. This also gives us a good barometer of the dogs' emotions—if either is too aroused by the sight of the other to eat really high value treats, it may not be wise to continue the introduction. If that's the case, we have a seat and hang out for a while to see if the dog can settle enough to show interest in food.

When both dogs appear reasonably calm and controlled, we drop leashes and let them greet each other naturally, without human interference. This is the nail-biting part—the first few nose-to-nose minutes of an introduction can make or break a relationship. We leave leashes on so if it does go poorly, we can separate the dogs easily, without being tempted to reach into the middle of the fray—a sure recipe for shredded human flesh. If this should occur, or if at any point in the introduction process, you see signs that there is more tension than goodwill, halt the session and either seek the assistance of a positive dog training/behavior professional, or seek out new playmates for both dogs.

If things are going well after a couple of moments, you can call up the dogs, remove both leashes, and let them resume play. As much as leaving leashes on is a safety measure, it's also a hazard. When dogs starting romping and rolling they can get tangled up in leashes, and *that* can trigger a fight! Once it's clear the dogs will play well together you can relax, but continue to keep an eye on them to be sure no one is getting aggravated. Then pull out those calendars and start scheduling play dates!

Most of the time this process works well. Dogs really are a social species and tend to get along reasonably well— as evidenced by the Potterfield Pooch Pool Plunge (PPPP) held every September here in Hagerstown, Maryland (and in a growing number of communities around the country). When the pool closes at the end of the summer, the last event is the PPPP—when people can bring their dogs to play together and swim in the pool. At our last plunge we had more than 100 dogs in attendance, most of them off leash, and nary a scuffle.

Introductions: The Millers Get a New Dog

Our pack of dogs is not the easiest in terms of introductions. Thus, when my husband, executive director of the local humane society, lost his heart to a red merle Australian Shepherd he encountered on a cruelty investigation, I knew we were in for some interesting introductions. Here's the cast of characters:

1. **Missy.** The newcomer, 8-year-old intact (unspayed) female red merle Australian Shepherd. Generally

appeasing nature, itchy skin (lower incisors worn to gums from chewing on herself)—had been in her latest home for three weeks; her prior owner had given her away at least two times previous to this and she had been returned both times. There were other dogs present at the farm where my husband found her and she seemed to get along with them. Her play style was unknown to us—Paul didn't see her actively interact with the other dogs.

2. **Katie**. 15-year-old spayed female geriatric, arthritic, cranky Australian Kelpie who growls and snaps at other dogs, but can't move very fast. She's a Cheerleader.

3. **Dubhy** (pronounced Duffy). 7-year-old neutered male Scottish Terrier with a history of being reactive/aggressive to other dogs. He usually has the final say on new dogs joining the Miller pack. He is a Chaser and will also Wrestle.

4. **Lucy**. 3-year-old spayed female Cardigan Corgi who combines a sweet, appeasing personality with aggressive assertiveness over valuable resources— space as well as food and coveted objects (toys). She prefers to play with humans, but will Wrestle with Bonnie, and reluctantly Tug.

5. **Bonnie**. 2-year-old spayed female Scottie/Corgi/ Something mix, sweet, appeasing, and offensive to no one. Even Katie the cranky Kelpie likes her. Bonnie is a Chaser and Wrestler, plays Keep Away with Lucy, and loves to Tug.

Missy—here to stay after successful introductions to the rest of the Miller pack.

Missy and Lucy

With multiple dogs, it's usually best to introduce the new dog to the others one at a time. I started with Missy in the training center, and we brought in Lucy, the Corgi. Their behavior at a distance was promising—relaxed and friendly, so we brought them closer together and dropped leashes. Things went well until Missy, who had been in our home less than one full day, started to resource guard *me*. As long as the two dogs were wandering around the training center together they were fine, but if they approached me, Missy would give a ferocious growl as she positioned herself between me and Lucy. Fortunately, Lucy chose not to take offense and the encounters didn't escalate. They didn't play, but neither did they fight.

Conclusion: Promising with management—potential for future relationship complications around resource guarding.

Missy and Bonnie

As expected, this introduction was completely uneventful. Missy growled at Bonnie once, but Bonnie's obviously deferent demeanor worked its magic. Missy was unconcerned. They also didn't play, but were quite relaxed with each other. In fact, they did so well we brought Lucy back in and let the three of them interact together.

Conclusion: All systems go—no anticipated problems.

Missy and Dubhy

This one worried me the most. I feared that if Missy growled at Dubhy the way she had at the two girls it could be disastrous. I brought Dubhy into the training center with Missy 40 feet away, in the middle of the room. The instant Dubhy saw her, he became tense—head up, hard eye contact, tail up, and wagging stiffly. I have done a significant amount of behavior modification with Dubhy's reactivity, so I began feeding him canned chicken to give him a positive association with Missy's presence. His body language softened and he returned to a less aroused state, able to respond to my cue for sit, down, and several other behaviors. We approached Missy until we were about three feet away and he continued to be somewhat tense, but repeatedly looking at her with a soft expression, and then looking back at me for more chicken. I took a deep breath and we unclipped leashes. Dubhy took a step toward Missy, stiffened, and with a loud snarl, launched himself toward her.

I stepped forward and gave him one shot of citronella spray from the can of Direct Stop/Spray Shield™ that I held in my hand. He stopped, looked at me, sneezed once, shook his head, and visibly relaxed. His body language softened, and his subsequent interactions with her were completely relaxed and non-confrontational. Fortunately Missy hadn't responded to his aggression with aggression of her own.

Conclusion: Cautiously optimistic.

Missy and Katie

Rather than make Katie trudge to the training center on failing legs, we introduced Missy to her in our back yard. Katie snapped at Missy as Missy passed by her on the back porch, but Missy ignored her and Katie didn't pursue her.

Conclusion: Promising, with management.

We then reintroduced Bonnie and Lucy, and finally Dubhy, to the group in the back yard, without incident. Dubhy passed under Missy's nose at the back door with nary a second glance. Missy had shown no desire to play with any of the Miller dogs (it turned out she's much happier playing with humans than with other dogs), but at least they were all getting along. If we were looking for an active playmate for any of our dogs, Missy wouldn't have been a good choice. But as simply a new companion for us, she had navigated the tricky waters of the Miller pack skillfully and successfully. Dog-human play (see Chapter 3) is every bit as desirable as dog-dog play. Missy was here to stay.

Breaking Up Fights

Sometimes, despite your best efforts, dog play turns into dogfight, whether it's an introduction that goes wrong, or play that turns ugly. Your first instinctive response may be to yell at the top of your lungs to try to break up the battle. Your second is often to reach in and attempt to bodily rescue your canine pal—especially if it appears he is getting the worst of it. Neither of these actions is likely to be effective. Yelling often adds fuel to the stress and arousal that led to the fight in the first place, and only intensifies the battle. Reaching into the fray more often than not results in multiple lacerations to human skin—sometimes inflicted by your own dog, who is too engaged in the battle to recognize or respect his own person's hand, arm, or face.

Of course, you can't just stand back and watch when a ferocious dogfight is in progress. So, what *should* you do?

Familiarize yourself with various tools and techniques that have the greatest chance of successfully quelling doggie disputes with the least injury to all parties. Then determine which are most appealing to you, and be sure to have them on hand (and in your head) should the time come when you need them.

These tools and techniques range from small and simple to big and bold. It is important to remember that none of them are foolproof; they all involve some inherent risk to the dogs who are fighting and to the humans who are trying to intervene, and they all can be applied with varying degrees of success. You will need to weigh the odds and decide, in each case, if the risk outweighs the potential for injury from the fight itself.

Aversives

Aversives are tools that a dog finds offensive to the senses—smells, sounds, and other stimuli that are strong enough to stop a behavior. In general, aversives can be most effective if used to interrupt fighting dogs prior to full arousal in an altercation. Their effectiveness decreases as arousal levels increase—although they may still succeed in stopping many full-scale fights. Aversives should also be considered primarily a tool for crisis intervention—they should not be used as basic training tools.

Blasting dogs with water from a nearby hose is a tried and true method of separating fighting dogs—assuming a hose happens to be nearby with a powerful enough spray to do the job. A good tool to keep in your arsenal for the right time and place.

One of the easily-portable aversive sprays, such as Direct Stop/Spray Shield ™ (citronella)—the one I used with Dubhy—or Halt!™ (pepper spray) might be an effective alternative to the hose. Of the two, Direct Stop/Spray Shield, available from Premier (www.gentleleader.com), is the safer choice, since pepper spray products are more corrosive, and the spray can drift and affect innocent bystanders—humans as well as dogs. There are laws in some jurisdictions requiring that users of pepper spray products complete a training course and carry a permit. In a pinch, even a fire extinguisher, while not easily portable, might just happen to be a handy and effective aversive tool.

Another option is a marine air horn. One trainer I know has an air horn that makes ten different sounds—sirens, horns, barnyard animals, etc., and she can crank the sound up to a deafening level. Air horns—available at boating supply stores—can be effective, but you risk damage to eardrums, both canine and human, and you do take a chance of frightening dogs beyond repair.

Other loud sounds can work too. A rape whistle (cover your own ears before you blow), dropping a stainless steel dog bowl on the floor, crashing two pan lids together like cymbals...any of these *might* work to interrupt a canine conflict.

Physical Intervention

Sometimes you do need to intervene physically. If you prepare in advance, you can build your own risk-reducing fight-interrupting tools. For example, you can attach a couple of handles to a sheet of plywood to make a "parting board" that you can lower between two sparring dogs to force them apart.

Dogfighters—and some Pit Bull owners who don't fight their dogs, but know the breed's potential—carry a "parting stick" or "break stick" with them wherever they go with their dogs. This is usually a carved or whittled hammer handle, tapered to a rounded point at one end. When two dogs are locked in combat, the parting stick can be forced between a dog's teeth and turned sideways, to pry open the jaws. Parting sticks can break a dog's teeth, and a dog whose jaws have just been "parted" may turn on the person doing the parting. Or, the dogs may just re-engage, unless someone immediately whisks the other dog to safety. Like many other techniques offered here, this method should only be considered for dire emergencies.

A blanket can also be a useful tool. Tossed over the fighters (one over each works best), it muffles outside stimuli, thereby reducing arousal. This also allows the humans to reach in and physically separate the combatants by picking up the wrapped pooches with less risk of a serious bite—the blanket will also cushion the effect of teeth on skin if the dog does whirl and bite.

Here's a somewhat drastic technique, reminding us that when a dog's life and limb are at stake, drastic measures may be called for. You can wrap a leash around the aggressor's neck or get hold of a collar and twist to cut off the dog's airflow, until he lets go to try to get a breath of air, then pull the dogs apart. Of course, this could be more difficult than it sounds. It might be a challenge to get a leash around the neck of a dog who is "attached" by the mouth to another dog without getting your hands in harm's way, and grabbing a collar to twist also puts hands in close proximity to teeth.

Here's one more approach to physical intervention; one that could be a little difficult if the aggressor is a 150-pound St. Bernard, but may be worth trying with a smaller dog. If you do decide to try this one, I suggest you use it only in a one-on-one dog brawl, and only if you have a second person with you who can corral the second dog when he breaks free; I would not recommend it in a multi-dog fight situation, or if you are alone: Lift the rear of the clearly-identified aggressor so that he is suspended with his fore-feet barely touching the ground. The dog lets go, and the target can scoot free. You might steer clear of this one for a dog who is human-aggressive; when the target dog scoots off, you could be the next target.

Now, all you need to do is stuff a canister of Direct Stop/Spray Shield in your pocket, attach a parting stick to your belt, hang a fire extinguisher over one arm, carry a blanket over your other arm, balance a sheet of plywood on your head, wear an air horn around your neck, be sure you have at least one friend with you, and you are ready for anything.

Seriously, if and when that fight happens, take a deep breath, resist your instincts to yell or leap in the middle of the fray, quickly review your available options, and choose the one—or ones—that are most likely to work in that place and time. When the fight is over and no one is being rushed to the hospital in an ambulance, remember to take a moment to relax and breathe, and then congratulate yourself for your quick thinking.

Chapter 3
IF YOU DON'T PLAY, YOU CAN'T WIN

HUMANS PLAYING WITH DOGS

Just like dogs have preferred dog-dog play styles, so do humans have play preferences with their dogs. The best match, of course is when a human's preferred play style is compatible with her dog's, but at least humans have a larger capacity for adapting their play to the style of the dog as needed.

Human-dog play styles generally fall into four categories:

- **Object Play**. This is play that centers around an object of some type—a toy, a ball, a stick. Dog and human both tend to focus more on the object than each other. Throw the Frisbee™. Toss the tennis ball. Chase the stick. Push the Jolly Ball™. Tug the rope toy. This type of play can be great physical exercise and a valuable part of a training program. Application for object play may be limited for dogs who have physical disabilities.

- **Mind Games**. These are perfect for the dog who is on enforced restricted activity due to physical limitations, recent surgery, apartment living, or a spell of bad weather. The good news is that mental exercise can be every bit as tiring as physical exercise: a dog who can do brain calisthenics can avoid the problem of kennel stress often experienced by dogs who must be on cage rest or house arrest.

- **Chase Games**. Play that involves chasing offers exercise benefits for both dog *and* human. Any games that encourage energetic physical activity require rules of conduct for the players. For example, its okay for the dog to chase you—however, he is not allowed to bite you, or your clothes.

- **Contact Play**. These are the truly rough physical games, and should be played with lots of caution. For some reason, it's more often (although not exclusively) male humans than female who enjoy body contact sports with their dogs. It's easy to reinforce inappropriate behaviors with rough play. Like Chasing, Contact Games should be played with very clear rules about which behaviors are allowed and which are not.

Regardless of a human's preferred canine games, as the species with the larger brain, we need to be able to adjust our play to the dog we're trying to play with. I do behavior assessments each week as a volunteer at our local shelter, and one piece of the assessment process requires us to play with the dog. A variety of staff and volunteers assist with assessments, and almost invariably the person doing the handling part of the process reaches for a toy to throw for the dog to initiate play. Perhaps because of our opposable thumbs,

Harley enjoys Object Play with owner/dog trainer Katie Ervin. Chasing Frisbees and Tug are two of his favorites.

object-play seems to be the first choice of a high percentage of humans.

Not so for the dogs! While occasionally a shelter dog's eyes light up at the bounce of a ball, the majority of dogs being assessed show little interest in the objects used to entice them to frolic—far more of them are willing to chase if the handler invites the dog to run after her around the assessment room. Some need to be gently coaxed to engage in play, and some simply seem to have no interest in playing whatsoever—either too busy looking out the windows, or too intimidated by the handler, the assessment process or the shelter environment for play to be a viable behavior option. For some dogs, the stress of the shelter environment clearly inhibits their willingness—or ability—to play. Others may have simply never learned *how* to play with people. For more on this, see Chapter 8.

This shelter dog needed to be gently coaxed to play.

While I don't have any scientific studies to back up my theory, I'd be willing to bet that the percentage of dogs who never learned to play is higher in the population of shelter dogs than in a corresponding population of dogs who've found their lifelong loving homes. Play is such a valuable bonding activity that dogs and owners who play well together are, I strongly believe, far more likely to find ways to stay together for a lifetime. Good motivation to read the chapters that follow and find new ways to play with your canine pal!

Chapter 4
Play It Again, Sam
The Benefits of Play

In addition to being just fun, there are several benefits to dogs who engage in play. These include:

- Play can be a way to get more exercise.

- Play can be used as a fun way to train your dog.

- Play can be used as part of a program to modify unwanted behavior in your dog.

Play to Exercise

A tired dog is a well-behaved dog. You'll hear this mantra in training centers around the world. As evidence of this, right now our five dogs, ranging in age from 2 to 15, are all peacefully sleeping on the floor—two at my feet under my desk, two in their crates with the crate doors open, and one on her bed in the living room. This doesn't happen by accident.

Our three older dogs, Dubhy, Missy and Katie, are 7, 8, and 15 respectively and easily settle into a snooze whenever the opportunity presents itself. But three-year-old Lucy the Cardigan Corgi and two-year-old Bonnie the Scottie/Corgi are another story. The two youngsters would pester me to

A tired dog is a well-behaved dog.

pieces, or perhaps tear the house to shreds, if they didn't get enough exercise.

We start at 6:00 a.m. with the barn routine. Dubhy, Missy, and Katie are content to amble about while we feed, turn horses out and clean stalls. Not so Bonnie and Lucy. Lucy's object of choice for barn play is a rubber Genuis™ toy (www.caninegenius.com). Shaped like a bowling pin, it bounces unpredictably when launched, and for the hour we're in the barn, husband Paul and I repeatedly launch it down the barn aisle—kicking it when Lucy drops it at our feet, throwing it when she puts it in our hands. Bonnie follows, although not with quite as much dedication, waiting for a lapse in Lucy's attention so she can grab the toy and entice Lucy into a game of Keep Away.

By the time we're done, Lucy is ready to collapse in happy exhaustion on the floor, and Bonnie's happy to call it a morning. I can return to the house and settle down at my computer for a few hours of peace. A couple of hours anyway. By 10:00 a.m. they're ready for another round. Lucy

The Miller dogs engage in morning barn play. Lucy tirelessly fetches her Genius toy while the other pack members scrounge bits of grain from the barn floor.

dances in my office doorway, eyes bright, her shrill herding dog voice ready to let loose if I ignore her obvious message. They all need a post-breakfast potty break anyway, so the pack troops outside and Lucy and Bonnie get another 10-minute session of chase the toy—this time the Fling Thing™ (www.westpawdesign.com)—a very durable, but soft foam disc-type toy. Again, Lucy prefers Object-Play with me, while Bonnie looks for opportunities to bite Lucy's heels or play Keep Away with Lucy's toy.

Our next play break is over lunch—a more relaxed half-hour while I eat, read a book, and toss the Fling Thing for Bonnie and Lucy. The other three hang out with me looking for ear-scratches and an occasional dog cookie. Depending on the day, some or all of the gang may join me for afternoon barn chores if I have a free evening, or entertain themselves in the backyard while I hustle through the feeding routine to get done in time to teach classes. Entertaining themselves in the backyard does little for exercise, however—Lucy, who suffers from mild separation distress, just sits by the back door waiting to get back in, and Bonnie lies on the grass under a tree.

On a really good day, the whole pack goes for a long hike around our 80-acre farm. I take advantage of Lucy's dedication to object-play by tossing a toy for her as we hike, getting extra mileage out of the experience. A hike takes the place of several backyard toy-tossing sessions.

It's probably true that the majority of dogs in this country are under-exercised. I realize that not every dog owner has a barn or an 80-acre farm to fulfill their dogs' exercise needs, but every dog owner has—or should have—the ability to devise indoor or backyard games that will serve the same purpose. And there are those days when inclement weather limits my willingness to toss toys in the backyard. Sorry Lucy, wild thunderstorms and zero degree weather don't do it for me. So we take it indoors.

You can object-play fetch games with your dog in a fenced yard, or for apartment dwellers and during bad weather, down a long hallway, or even up and down a set of carpeted stairs. *Note: Long-backed dogs such as Dachshunds and Corgis and other dogs with or prone to back problems should not play on stairs, and stairs without carpeting are too slippery to be safe for play for any dog.* You and your dog can Tug to your heart's content in the comfort of your own living room. Mind games (such as shaping) are great for limited space play/exercise even if you and/or your dog are on restricted activity due to physical limitations. There really is no excuse not to play with your dog.

Play to Exercise Games

Hide and Seek

Have one person hide in the woods. With your dog on a long line—or off leash if he's off-leash reliable—cue him to "Find Joe!" (insert appropriate name) and let him start looking. At first Joe can help by calling your dog's name from his hiding place, or making other noises as "hints." Eventually your dog won't need the hints.

King of the Mountain, Version 1

As you hike with your dog in the woods and fields, give him extra exercise mileage by encouraging him to jump up on fallen logs, tree stumps, rock piles. He gets to be the King.

Kaiya's version of King of the Mountain involves climbing trees.

King of the Mountain, Version 2

As you hike with your dog, climb a tall hill, stand at the top and throw his ball down the hill for him to fetch. He gets the extra exercise mileage of climbing the hill over and over, and you get to be the King. I used this one very successfully with Keli, my first, very high-energy Australian Kelpie.

The Miller dogs prefer King of the Haystack.

Play to Train

There are volumes written on the subject of play-training. In fact, play has become such a popular training tool (and an excellent one) that some folks have forgotten the joy of playing just for the sake of playing! Still, it's worth addressing here, at least briefly, since one of the advantages of play-training is that it reminds owners that training is supposed to be fun.

Training is simply the process of reinforcing desired behaviors and preventing your dog from being reinforced for unwanted ones so that the desired behaviors will be more likely to happen and the unwanted ones less likely. Since all living things repeat behaviors that are rewarding to them, this prescription works well, if used consistently, to train your dog to do the things you want him to do.

Remember that rewards are in the eye of the receiver. Play only works as a reward for training if you're good at figuring out—and delivering—the kind of play your dog likes. If your idea of play is to thump your dog on his ribcage, but he's sensitive about being touched, you actually punish, rather than reward, when you "play" with him. You will decrease the likelihood of the behavior being repeated that elicited your rib-thumps.

Play has been incorporated into training for quite some time. Trainers were willing to use play in training long before they accepted the use of food as a reinforcer for training. Thirty-plus years ago, my trainer taught me to toss a ball between my legs to get a fast, happy recall. It worked. I happened to be training a ball-crazy Kelpie at the time. If I'd been working with Dubhy, the Scottish Terrier who's part of our current family, it wouldn't have helped at all—he could care less about tennis balls. Today, the well-equipped trainer has a large selection of toys and games to choose from—balls, tug toys, squeakies, plush toys, and physical play. And as the line between play and training blurs even further, the behaviors we teach become games and reinforcers in and of themselves. Targeting—the behavior of touching a designated body part to a designated spot—is a highly reinforcing behavior/game to many dogs.

I was reminded once again of the value of play in training during one of my advanced classes recently. We were practicing recalls in class, where our goal is to get a consistent, reliable, super-enthusiastic, super-speedy response to the important recall cue. Karin, with her blue merle Border Collie, Kip, is a master at using play to train. She plans to compete with him in Agility, a canine sports venue that encourages play-training as a way to keep the dogs upbeat and energetic about running courses. Karin uses a variety of reinforcers when she calls Kip to "Come!" including turning and running away from him so he can play the "Chase!" game. His favorite, however, is a rousing game of "Tug!" when he gets to her. Kips recall is delightful, and Karin is proud of the fact that he whirled and came back to her recently when called away from a running deer.

While play-training has become a lot more sophisticated over the years, the principle is the same: behaviors that are reinforced increase. Because there are times when you can't use food, or don't have it with you, or times when your dog is too full or too stressed to eat; because there are times when you'd just prefer not to use food for training purposes; and because using play as a reinforcer is just plain fun, there is huge value in figuring out how to use toys and games in your dog's training program.

Here are some examples. I'm assuming that the examples given are reinforcing to the hypothetical dog in each

Dog trainer Karin Fellers is a master at using play to train her blue-merle Border Collie, Kip.

scenario. Remember to select the examples (and think up more of your own) that incorporate a form of play that is reinforcing to your dog.

Play to Train Games

Reinforcing "Sit!"

1. Ask your dog to sit, and when he does, say "Yes!" and pull a tug toy out from your jacket for a rousing game of tug. Do several repetitions and watch your dog sit more and more enthusiastically when he hears your "Sit!" cue. (The "Yes!" is a verbal reward marker to let your dog know what behavior has earned the reinforcer.)

Dog owner Leanne Buzzell uses a toy to reinforce "sit-stay" with her Australian Shepherds, Izzi and Rebel.

2. Ask your dog to sit and when he does, say "Yes!" and pull a tennis ball out of your pocket to throw for him to fetch.

3. Ask your dog to sit and when he does, say "Yes!" and invite him to leap into the air to touch his nose to your hand.

Reinforcing "Down!"

1. Ask your dog to down and when he does, say "Yes!" and play "patty-paws" with him.

2. Ask your dog to down and when he does, say "Yes!" and bounce around with him.

Reinforcing "Come!"

1. Call your dog to come and when he starts running toward you, say "Yes!" and then turn and run away for a game of "Chase Me!"

2. Call your dog to come and when he reaches you and sits in front of you, squeak a plush toy and throw it for him to chase.

3. Call your dog to come and when he reaches you and sits, toss him a crumpled up paper towel to shred.

4. Hide behind a tree when your dog isn't looking. Call him to come and when he finds you, say "Yes!" and roll around in the grass with him to celebrate.

Reinforcing "Heel"

1. Cue your dog to heel and after he's taken several steps alongside you, say "Yes!" and then turn and run away fast.

2. Cue your dog to heel and after he's taken several steps with you, squeak a small squeaky toy in your pocket. Do this randomly during heeling, and every once in a while follow the squeaks with a toss of the toy for him to chase.

3. Cue your dog to heel and after he's walked with you for a bit, tell him "Yes!" then "Find it!" and run to a spot where you've hidden a favorite toy. Let him find it and play with it.

Play to Modify Behavior

Play is hugely valuable as a tool for modifying behavior, both for operantly conditioned behaviors and classically conditioned ones. With operant behaviors, the dog consciously chooses to perform a behavior in order to influence the consequence of his actions.

Operant conditioning works in four ways:

1. **Positive Reinforcement.** The dog's behavior makes a good thing happen; as a result the dog's future offering of this behavior increases. A dog's main mission in life is to make good stuff happen!

2. **Positive Punishment.** The dog's behavior makes a bad thing happen; as a result the dog's future offering of this behavior decreases. Dogs don't like bad stuff to happen!

3. **Negative Punishment.** The dog's behavior makes a good thing go away; as a result the dog's future offering of this behavior decreases. Dogs want good stuff to stick around!

4. **Negative Reinforcement.** The dog's behavior makes a bad thing go away; as a result the dog's future offering of this behavior increases. Dogs want bad stuff to go away!

Examples of operantly conditioned behaviors include:

• Dog runs into his crate at bedtime because he knows "running into crate" makes a cookie happen (positive reinforcement).

• Dog barks at the mail carrier because he knows (or thinks he knows) that barking makes the mail carrier go away (negative reinforcement).

• Dog hands you his tennis ball and sits because he knows "sit" makes you throw the ball again (positive reinforcement).

You can use play to operantly modify unwanted behaviors by teaching your dog a play behavior that's incompatible with the one you don't want. Here are two examples.

Greeting Visitors at the Door

Bouncer jumps all over your guests when they enter your home. He loves people, and he settles down nicely after the initial greeting, so you hate to put him away when you have visitors. Instead of banishing him from the fun, set a basket of toys outside your front door, with instructions for your visitor to pick one, enter the home and toss the toy for Bouncer to fetch. When he brings it back to your guest, he's more likely to sit for the friend to toss the toy again (especially if you've taught him this) than jumping on the person.

Go Wild and Freeze

Thanks go out to trainer September Morn, who I believe was the originator of this game that's now a mainstream play activity for many positive trainers. This is great for dogs who love overly-rough physical play with humans. Say "Go wild!" and start playing with Rowdy, encouraging him to be physical. When he starts getting too aroused say "Freeze!" then stop playing, stand up straight, fold your arms, and refuse to play until he settles into a sit or down. If he won't stop, step over a baby gate as you say "Freeze!" When he settles, invite him to "Go Wild!" again. Do lots of repetitions until he responds promptly to the "Freeze!" cue.

With classically conditioned behaviors, the dog's brain has made an association between two stimuli—an initially neutral one and a hardwired one to which he has an innate emotional and/or physiological response. The neutral one takes on the meaning of the hardwired one. Examples of classically conditioned behaviors include:

• The click of the clicker makes your dog's head swivel in your direction and his eyes light up (and he's salivating, even if you can't see it). His brain has associated the click sound with food.

• The presence of a small child causes your dog to stiffen and growl. His brain has associated children with having his fur pulled and his nose poked.

• When you pick up your dog's leash, he leaps and dances joyfully. His brain has associated the sight of his leash with lovely walks in the park.

You can use play to modify behaviors through classical conditioning if your dog enjoys a particular toy or game. The goal is to associate something the dog has a negative opinion of with the pleasurable play experience.

This process of changing the association is called counter-conditioning. Presenting the stimulus—the behavior trigger—at a low level of intensity first, until the dog accepts it, and gradually increasing the intensity of the stimulus, is called desensitization. The two are most effective if used together in programs we call counter-conditioning and desensitization, or CC&D.

One common application of play-related CC&D to behavior modification is with dogs who are storm sensitive. Storm-phobias are notoriously difficult to modify, in part because there are so many stimuli associated with a storm (sound of thunder, flashes of lightning, rain on the roof, wind in the trees, change in barometric pressure) and because it's impossible to control the intensity of stimulus with real storms. You can acquire a thunder CD and play it at a low volume while feeding high-value treats, gradually increasing the volume until its full intensity. You can turn your sprinkler on and aim it at your roof to simulate rain, and feed treats. You can rent a Hollywood wind machine and turn it on low to blow through your leaves, and feed treats. You can set up big spotlights outside and flash them on and off, and feed treats. For barometric pressure… you're on your own.

Or, you can try play. As soon as you are aware of a storm in the distance (often your storm-sensitive dog will *tell* you), grab your dog's favorite toy and start a rousing round of play. Tug is an especially good game for giving your dog a positive association with storms, because so many dogs experience such a high level of enjoyment with the Tug game. Even if the storm eventually reaches an intensity where she will no longer play because she's too stressed, there's a good likelihood that your dog will become more storm-resilient over time, and more able to tolerate higher levels of storm intensity, if you keep associating them with Tug. Be sure to play with her often enough at non-storm times that your dog doesn't start to think Tug *makes* storms happen!

At my Peaceable Paws training center, a client of mine tried another application of counter-conditioning play with her dog-reactive Briard with great success. Grandy's reactivity was great enough that if Nicole tried to work with him on her own back deck when the neighbor's dog was out, he was too stressed to take treats. Nicole decided to try play, and discovered that a two-minute gentle, controlled game of Tug was enough to reduce her dog's stress enough that he was willing to take treats and proceed with a more traditional CC&D program using high value treats.

Chapter 5

LET THE GAMES BEGIN

PLAYING WITH YOUR DOG

It's time to get serious about having fun with your dog. The games offered in the following pages were gathered from dog owners worldwide as well as from my own experience, and are quite eclectic. Your job is to figure out which ones appeal to your dog (and to you!) and to start playing. In some cases your dog will take to the game immediately, in others you may need to teach him how to play—teach him the rules. Some simply won't be suited to your dog—or to you. Remember that the whole point of playing games is to have fun, so don't let yourself get *too* serious when teaching play and play rules, and certainly not when playing!

There are some games that come with cautionary notes because they may not be appropriate for some dog and human players. It's also your job to determine if those cautions apply to you and/or your dog. If your dog has been play-deprived, doesn't know how to play, or doesn't catch on to these games easily, don't give up—proceed to Chapter 8 for help on teaching your dog to play.

Now get ready to have fun!

Find It Games

It was no surprise to me that by far the most frequently-mentioned game suggested by dog trainers and owners during my research for this chapter was some version of "Find It!" This seems to be an activity that is almost universally appreciated by canines and humans alike. (See the "Thanks" secion at the end of the book for the complete list of dog-lovers who contributed play ideas.)

What did surprise me was the creativity with which the humans developed variations of the game. Here are several versions:

Basic "Find It"

Leave your dog on a sit-stay (or have someone hold his leash, or close him in a separate room) and hide a treat or toy. Return to your dog and tell him "Find it!"

To teach this game, start with a dozen yummy treats and your dog in front of you. Say "Find it!" in an excited voice and toss one treat off to the side. Be sure he sees you toss it. As soon as he eats that one, toss another in the opposite direction and say "Find it!" again. Keep doing this, tossing treats back-and-forth, until your dozen treats are gone.

Now leave your dog on a "Wait!" or "Stay," toss a treat 10-15 feet out, and release him with an excited "Find it!" Repeat this a half-dozen times, then leave him on a wait or stay while you walk 10-15 feet out, place a treat on the floor, return to him, pause (so he doesn't think your return is the cue to release), and release him with your "Find it!" Repeat a half-dozen times.

Next, let him watch you "hide" treats in harder places—behind a table leg, on a chair seat, under a paper bag… Each time you hide a treat, return, pause, and release him with your "Find it!" cue to go get the treat.

When he's doing very well with that step, make it more difficult for him to see exactly where you hide the treat, by blocking his view with your body as you hide it, or hiding it where a piece of furniture impedes his view. Now he *really* has to start looking for it. This is the beginning of the real fun. Remember to keep the tone of your "Find it!" cue happy and excited! Your dog will start using his incredible sense of smell to find the treat, and you'll get to watch and learn how to read him when he's "on scent."

During this part of the game, you may be tempted to help him find the treat if he doesn't find it right away. *Be careful!* It's okay to indicate the general area, but don't find the treat for him—he may learn to just wait for you to show him rather than working to find it himself. If you have a dog who's very toy-motivated you can switch to hiding toys, or make it variable—sometimes hide a toy, sometimes a treat. When I taught my Corgi this game, I started using cow hooves when we got to this point.

As soon as he's figured out how to find the hidden treat or toy using his nose, you can increase the challenge by putting him in another room when you hide it. Wipe the object on a clean gauze pad first, and then hide it. When you bring your dog back into the room, hold the gauze pad in front of his nose and say, "Find it," and then let him look. (Again, you can indicate the general area at first, if necessary, to help him get started, but don't help too much!) Allowing your dog to sniff the pad tells him what scent he's looking for. Alternatively, you can name the object prior to this stage and use the name to tell him what he's looking for, as in "Find the cow hoof!" The gauze pad method gives you more flexibility to have him look for new objects in the future that you haven't pre-named for him.

Find and Destroy

Put the "Find it!" object in a container to be found and "opened" (destroyed) by the dog.

Put treats in an empty cardboard container destined for recycling—an oatmeal cylinder; a small, sturdy cardboard box; paper towel tube; etc. Have him wait or stay and show him the container, shaking it—with drama added: "Oooooh, what's this? What've I got?" Have him wait while you hide the container in another room, then return to him, pause, and tell him to "Find it!" Follow him and have fun watching as he gleefully shreds the container to get the goodies inside.

Caution: If your dog eats cardboard you may choose not to encourage this behavior, or at least you will want to retrieve the cardboard shreds before he ingests copious amounts.

Find the Human

Have your dog find a hidden *person*.

There are several different ways to play this game. You can have your dog wait while *you* hide from him, or just duck behind a bush or tree when he isn't looking. If your dog is very connected to you, maybe even has a little separation distress, he may start looking for you as soon as he realizes you're gone. If not, you can jump-start the game by calling him to "Come!" when you've hidden yourself. When he finds you, have a big celebration—make a fuss and feed yummy treats or let him play with a favorite toy. Gradually fade (take away) the come cue to encourage him to look for you on his own, without being called.

Or, you can have your dog stay with you while someone else hides, and tell him "Find (insert appropriate name here)." When he finds the person, have them celebrate with the dog, and then send him back to you, where you reward him with treats and toys. Teaching him to return to you after he finds someone is useful if the two of you ever want to try your hand-and-paw at Search and Rescue work—either informal or formal.

When he's good at finding people in simple hiding places, you can make it harder—hide in a shower stall, crawl under the bed, climb up a tree...

Caution: Play this game in a safely enclosed area unless your dog has a really reliable recall. Also, some dogs panic when they can't find their humans, if you are hiding from your dog, keep an eye on him to make sure he doesn't go on a long journey through the woods in his panic to find you.

Find Treats in Tub

Dog finds treats tossed in a tub of toys.

This one's as simple as it sounds, and is great for keeping your dog busy for awhile. Put all his toys in a tub (small child's swimming pool works for this), then toss a handful of treats in with the toys (mix them all around to make it harder), and let him search for them.

Find a Treat in My Hand

Dog figures out which hand holds the treat.

Another simple one—this game is great when you and your dog can't play run-around games. Let him see you put a treat in one hand, then put your hands behind your back, and swap the treat back-and-forth. Sometimes end up with the treat in the original hand, sometimes in the other. Then bring your hands in front of you at his nose level with your fists close, and let him indicate with his nose or paw which fist holds the treat.

Value of Find It Games

"Find it" is a simple behavior that even play-challenged dogs can perform with relative ease. It's tons of fun! And it can also have useful applications, such as finding your lost keys, the TV remote, or a missing pet or person. Sometimes Timmy really does fall in the well!

Running Games

Dogs are hardwired to run after things that move. Many canine companions naturally engage in chase games. According to Mary Bailey and John Burch in their excellent book *How Dogs Learn*, exercise is a primary reinforcer—something that has innate value to your dog. This means that just running around is very rewarding to him. This should come as no huge surprise to dog owners, most of whom have had the fun of seeing their dogs with the zoomies—also known as puppy rushing or frapping (FRenetic Activity Period). There's no mistaking the wild joy on the dog's face as he zooms around at high speeds, often with his tail end tucked.

Caution: Be careful with running games in hot weather, with bracycephalic (short-faced) dogs, and with dogs who have any kind of physical limitations such as arthritis, obesity, or other medical conditions. Remember to check with your veterinarian before engaging your dog in vigorous physical activity to which he's unaccustomed.

Here are some ways you can capitalize on "Running" as play.

Running Together

Dog and human run side-by-side.

Running doesn't have to mean chasing. Niles, a 5-year-old Pug from Saratoga Springs, New York, loves running alongside his human, dog trainer Cynthia Chelsea Koslow. She uses it as a reinforcer for polite leash walking. After a good stretch of leash walking she'll say, "Let's run!" and both

Helen Fine and her Golden Retriever, Daisy, run side-by-side.

dog and owner take off for a short sprint. She also used it to modify his car chasing behavior—having him sit while the car passes and then doing a short run. Niles has learned to anticipate the fun of the run after the sit, which is *incompatible* with chasing the car—he can't do both at the same time. Koslow says, "The running together is so much fun for him, and for me—it's a real bonding experience each time we do it. The joy on his face is wonderful to see."

Run the Bases

Running together with a goal in mind—to run the bases on a ball field.

My friend and fellow positive trainer, Laura Dorfman of Glencoe, Illinois, plays this one with her Terrier mix, Kaiya. Part of the game is that dog and player have to touch each of the bases as they pass. Laura says:

As I took Kaiya on her birthday walk the other day we did our favorite base-running routine of starting at home plate and running all the bases until we get back to home. This last time as Kaiya got to home plate she missed it and I called her back and said, 'Kaiya, touch!' With her right front paw she slapped the plate, turned around and walked toward the dugout. I never pass a ball field with any dog without running the bases.

Monkey in the Middle; a Game the Whole Family Can Play

Dog runs back-and-forth between two humans who are tossing a toy/ball back-and-forth.

This is a perfect game for dogs who like to chase flying objects, even dogs who don't retrieve, and great for the family because there's no limit to the number of human players. You can also play with more than one dog, if they're compatible and no one gets guardy.

Humans stand some distance apart—in a circle if there are three or more—and throw the toy/ball to each other randomly. Dog chases the toy/ball, and occasionally gets to have it, either if someone drops it, or one human decides to throw it for her. This provides great exercise for the dog, without worrying about the retrieve part of a fetch game. Positive trainer Gina Crimmons of Bartlett, Illinois, plays this game with her dogs Tess and Riley. Tess doesn't retrieve, but loves to chase. Riley loves both chase and fetch. Crimmons says, "I miss a lot (hee hee) so then Riley will go get it and bring it back. He *seriously loves* this game, and is a high energy Jack Russell Terrier, so it's a great way for him to get some good exercise."

Value of Running Games

Exercise, exercise, exercise (for *both* of you!) and, like all the best games, relationship building. You can use running to teach a good *recall* (come) response.

Chasing Games

Another very popular activity with both species, Chasing is a variation of the Running Game. Instead of running *with* your dog, one of you is chasing the other.

Gimme That Thang

Known more familiarly as "Keep Away," in this game your dog gets to grab a toy or other object, and run away as you chase her. Of course some dogs do this with "forbidden objects"—things they are not supposed to have. That's not the game here—the worst thing you can do when your dog has a forbidden object is to chase him to try to take it away. With the "Gimme" game, you either offer your dog a "legal" play object or notice that he already has one, and start the game with a specific cue, such as "Gimme that!" and the chase is on.

Sometimes a little music can add to the spirit of the game. Laura Dorfman plays this one with her dog Star, described as follows:

> We call this game 'Gimme That Ball,' and it has a musical theme—sung to the tune of Gimme That Thang, circa 1970. It can be initiated by either Star or me. If she wants to play she walks over to the ball and looks cute. If I want to play I say in a very animated voice, 'Where's your ball? Gimme that ball!' The game begins with me starting to sing and Star takes off with her ball around the yard. I chase her and anticipate her moves and try to cut her off as

she runs by me. The whole thing is done to music (me singing). When I slow down the song she slows down running, and when I get louder and faster she speeds up. The game ends when the song stops and we usually collapse on the ground together from exhaustion.

Caution: Don't play this game until you have taught your dog to "Give" you an object from his mouth when you ask for it. When you do play, stop occasionally and ask your dog to "Give" or "Drop" the toy—trading for a treat if she needs a little extra incentive to give it up. Then start the game again with your "Gimme" cue. The cue will help your dog understand that you're playing a game, and the occasional "Give" break will ensure that you can get things away from her when you really need to.

Tag

This game is similar to "Gimme," but without the object in the dog's mouth. Human assumes a position that cues the dog that the game is on. Sometimes this is a "mock threat" position—legs apart, arms raised, intense, stalking toward the dog. The dog takes the hint and darts playfully away, with human in hot pursuit. Fran Dauster of Grand Bay, Alabama uses a verbal "You're it!" cue with her Dobermans to start a game of Tag.

Julie Sontag, a New York City trainer, cues up her dog's game of tag with a preamble of "Be a Dog." She gets on all fours, pants, and hops around, and then does a play bow by dropping her elbows to the ground and sticking her derriere in the air. Her dog returns the bow and she jumps up and gives chase, running from room to room, "almost" catching him. They run around coffee tables, up and off the bed, around obstacles and chairs. When her dog hides under the coffee table, she runs to another room and he chases her, then she spins around and chases him again. "It's a grand game," Julie says, "with lots of panting at the end."

Round Robin Recall (RRR)

Okay, this one is a training game as well as being lots of fun. Part of the fun is that you can have multiple human players. Start with everyone standing in a circle at least 15 feet in diameter. Take turns calling your dog in an excited voice. The person who calls the dog turns and runs away as soon as the dog looks in her direction, continues to make excited noises, even squeaking a squeaky toy if necessary to get the dog romping in pursuit. When the dog reaches the caller he gets a treat, or a short game of tug with the toy, then the next person calls the dog and runs away. The RRR game is great exercise for the humans as well as the dogs!

Caution: I don't recommend this game for dogs who get over-stimulated by chasing humans, especially when chasing triggers nipping, biting, or hard jumping.

Chase Stuff

Humans have long capitalized on a dog's natural instinct to chase things that move. Of course, the classic objects to chase are flying discs and tennis balls, but the possibilities for chase games are endless. Here are some more fun "Chase Stuff" games:

- Blow bubbles for your dog to chase.

- Spray water from a hose, a sprinkler, a squirt gun, and let your dog chase it.

- Tie a toy on the end of a longe whip (horse training equipment) or fishing pole for your dog to chase.

• Let him chase remote control cars, trucks, or helicopters. *Note: If your dog likes to destroy things you may lose your remote control toy to his teeth...*

• Shine a flashlight beam on the ground and encourage your dog to chase it.

Caution: Some dogs who chase flashlight beams (or laser lights) get so intense about it, that it turns into a very difficult, even debilitating obsessive compulsive disorder called "light chasing" or "shadow chasing." If you have a high-intensity dog who is prone to over-stimulation, or your dog is not high intensity, but he seems to get highly aroused or fixated by light beams, I don't recommend encouraging him to play with light beams.

Value of Chase Games

Provides an acceptable outlet for dogs' hardwired instinct to chase things that move; offers excellent opportunities for exercise—even when you can't run (object-chasing games). You can use chase games to teach a good recall.

Digging Games

Digging is another hardwired, natural dog behavior that can be turned into a game. In fact, making it a game is one way of redirecting undesirable digging into an acceptable outlet—and making it fun for the human as well as the dog!

I like to call this game, "Diggety Dawg." Start by creating a digging place for your canine excavator. This can just be a clearly designated spot in your yard (mark the corners or edges in some way to indicate the perimeter), or you can use a digging box; build one yourself, or find a suitable child's sandbox. Dig up the spot in your yard so the dirt is reasonably soft and diggable, or fill the digging box with soft dirt. Now encourage your dog to dig in his personal dirt by semi-burying stuffed Kongs™, chew-bones, and other valuable toys. Let him see you bury them, then give him his digging cue (I like "Dig it!") and let him go to town.

If your dog needs encouragement to dig, get down and dirty—dig with him! Show him the treat or toy, tease him with it a little to get him excited, and half-bury it. Then start digging—with enthusiasm!—right next to the coveted object, and see if he doesn't start helping. Continuing playing "Diggety" with him until he catches on.

You can keep this game fun and unpredictable by burying great things in his digging pit when he's not watching, and letting him find them later. If he never knows what he might find there, but knows he'll often find great stuff, he's more likely to keep going back to it—instead of your flower beds.

You can also build excitement for digging by having him "Wait" or "Stay"—or using a tether if his wait/stay behaviors aren't reliable—and letting him watch you bury his favorite things. Then return to him, hold his collar, and ask him, "Want to dig? Want to dig?" in a very excited voice. Then say "Dig it!" and release him to go have fun.

Of course, if you're teaching your dog this game because he's already doing undesirable digging, you'll need to manage his access to areas where he's been digging in the past. Put temporary fencing around planting beds and other inviting areas while you reprogram his digging preference to his own personal digging spot.

Value of Digging Games

Provides an acceptable outlet for dogs' hardwired digging behavior. He can help you dig holes when you need them (and find buried treasure!).

Tug Games

The game of Tug has an undeserved bad rap in some training circles, while others, most notably the Agility world, have fully embraced it as an excellent activity to create focus and high arousal. Those two extremes aside, it's a great game just because it's fun, many dogs adore it, it's the perfect play activity for human family members who might otherwise want to get inappropriately physical with the dog, and it's a terrific energy-burner.

One of the most commonly-heard myths about playing Tug is that it makes the dog "dominant." There is so much misinformation passed around about hierarchy in dogs—this is just another log on the fire. If you *are* concerned about what Tug might do to your relationship with your dog, just remember that the definition of *leader* is "the one who controls the good stuff," and orchestrate your Tug-play accordingly.

I'm solidly in the pro-Tug camp. I strongly recommend setting rules for canine and human players of the game to protect against the possibility of reinforcing unwanted behaviors, but with those in place, you and your dog can Tug to your hearts' content. The rules are general guidelines for making Tug a positive training/relationship experience. The calmer and better-behaved your dog is, the less necessary it is to follow them strictly. The more rowdy and out of control your dog, the more closely you will want to adhere to them. By the way, don't be alarmed by your dog's growls during Tug—it's all part of the game. As long as his other behaviors are appropriate, let him growl his heart out!

Rule #1: You start the game. Keep the Tug toy put away, and get it out when you want to play. It's perfectly okay to get it out when you know he is in the mood, but it's your choice to start the game. You control the good stuff.

Rule #2: No grabbing. Hold up the toy, and if Bruiser grabs or leaps for it, say "Oops!" and hide it behind your back. Then offer it again. When Bruiser is no longer leaping or grabbing, say "Take It" and offer his end to him. Then give him the cue to "Tug!" or "Pull!" and the game is on. You control the good stuff and allow him to have it out of the goodness of your heart.

Rule #3: You win most of the time. "Winning" means you have the toy and Bruiser doesn't. At first, you may need to offer him an irresistible treat as you say, "Give!" He'll have to drop the toy to eat the treat, and you've won! As soon as he devours the treat, say "Take It!" again and offer him his end of the toy. Now he got *two* rewards for letting go of it—he got the treat, and he gets the toy back again! At least, he gets *his* end of the toy back. Practice the "Give" part of the game numerous times during each play session. Eventually you will be able to fade the use of the treat, as Bruiser realizes that the reward for "Give!" is more Tug. You control the good stuff.

Rule #4: Tug side-to-side only. Up and down tugging presents a risk of injury to the spine, and is more likely to loosen teeth. Even with side-to-side tugging, be sure you use an amount of force appropriate to your dog's size and personality. Tiny Toy breeds should Tug only very gently.

Rule #5: Use Time-outs as needed. If Bruiser gets too aroused and/or is putting his mouth on you or your clothing, use a cheerful "Too Bad, Time-Out!" when his arousal level starts to escalate to an unacceptable level, or the *instant* his teeth touch forbidden surfaces. Put the toy high on a shelf and sit down for a few minutes. Then if you want, retrieve the toy and play again. If you have a dog who allows his teeth to stray into forbidden territory frequently by creeping his jaws up the length of the toy, use a tug object with a clear demarcation near his end of the toy—a change in texture or material—and do a time-out immediately anytime his teeth cross that line. You control the good stuff, and Bruiser's inappropriate behavior makes the good stuff go away.

Rule #6: Supervise Children. Very young children should not play Tug with Bruiser unless, and until, the dog is impeccable about his self-control, and then only under direct supervision. Middle to older children can play with moderate supervision *if* they can be relied on to play by the rules, and *if* Bruiser is under reasonable self-control and not likely to get into trouble. Children can control the good stuff too! Adults who can't play by the rules should be forbidden to play.

Tucker, our Cattle Dog mix, loved to play Tug with my husband, Paul.

Rule #7: You end the game. You get to decide when Tug is over. End the game with a "Give—All Done!" cue and put the toy away on a high shelf or in a secure drawer. It'll be there, ready and waiting, when you decide to play again. You control the good stuff.

Tug toys can come in all shapes, sizes, colors and materials, but the best ones have these characteristics in common:

- They are long enough that your dog's teeth stay far away from your hand.

- They are made of a substance that invites your dog to grab and hold, and won't easily cause damage to teeth and gums.

- They are sturdy enough to withstand significant abuse.

- The "human end" has a comfortable handle or is otherwise easy to maintain a grip on.

- They are good value for the cost.

Value of Tug Games

An excellent way to redirect a "mouthy" dog's teeth to an appropriate object. Great exercise and the perfect outlet for family members who want to play roughly.

Mind Games

Mind games exercise your dog mentally rather than physically. Some people are surprised to discover that mental exercise can be every bit as tiring as physical exercise. I remember when we first got computers (a long time ago!) at the Marin Humane Society in California, where I worked for 20 years: I would go home exhausted after sitting behind my desk all day trying to stretch my brain around the totally

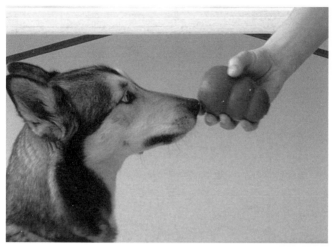

This shelter dog is being introduced to the joys of a stuffed Kong toy.

alien concepts. It's just as tiring for your dog to use his brain, especially if he's not accustomed to thinking hard.

Many methods of training don't require the dog to think as much as react. The more you routinely "help" your dog solve training problems, the less he has to think. Older training methods that use physical assistance, force, and/or corrections teach the dog avoidance behaviors rather than problem-solving skills. Modern training methods that reinforce the dog for experimenting and reward him for making the right decisions encourage mental exercise and develop problem-solving abilities.

Mind games blur the line between training and play—you often have a behavior goal in mind when you play them. That's perfectly okay. The dog will have fun—and see it as a game even if he's being trained—as long as *you* remember to have fun and see it as a game.

Interactive Toys

The new dog training paradigm has spawned a whole new generation of interactive toys. One of the best dog inventions in the last 50 years is the Kong™—a hard, hollow rubber toy shaped like a beehive, with a large opening in one end and a small hole in the other. Originally developed in the early 1980's as a fetch toy, it's now highly valued as a stuffing toy.

To stuff your dog's Kong, set it upside down in a mug, small end down, stuffing end up. If your dog is a Persistent Pete, stuff tightly so he has to work hard to empty it. Use his regular dinner kibble, moistened with chicken broth and then frozen, to give him a refreshing pup-sicle on a hot summer day. A cube of freeze-dried liver wedged under the lip can make it even more challenging to empty. Baby carrots also wedge neatly into a medium Kong, with squeeze cheese, peanut butter or cream cheese to fill the gaps. If your dog is more of a Softy Sue, stuff less firmly, so she doesn't just give up. Fresh fruits and veggies (no grapes, raisins or onions please!), dog cookies, bits of meat—anything your dog can eat is stuffing material.

Creative dogs learn to pick up their Kongs and drop them on the ground to make the treats fall out.

With the raging popularity of the Kong, more treat-dispensing toys continuously appear on the scene. The Buster Cube™ is a sturdy, hollow cube made of hard plastic with a hole on one side, designed by a Danish animal behaviorist. Fill the cube with treats, place it on the floor, and watch your dog push it around to make the treats fall out. Games that involve acquiring treats are usually quite popular with canines, and they seem to enjoy working for their food. In fact, some people routinely feed their dogs' entire meals this way.

On the same principle as the Buster Cube, but somewhat easier for dogs to figure out, are toys like the Roll-A-Treat Ball™, the Molecule Ball™, and the Tricky Treat Ball™. Since balls roll more easily than cubes, they can be a better choice than the Buster Cube for dogs who are less active, less assertive, or less persistent. The Dog Pyramid™ is an interesting variation of the cube/ball concept: the red rubber toy sits upright with the treat-hole at the top, and the weighted bottom prevents it from being knocked all the way over. It wobbles far enough for treats to fall out, but your dog has to work at it.

There are treat-dispensing toys that are even more sophisticated than Cubes and Balls. If your dog is bored with just rolling things around, try these:

- **Dog Twister™**. Requires your dog to locate the hidden treats by moving the interlocked segments around the circular puzzle in different directions with either his nose or paw. To increase the difficulty, various segments can be locked in position with the accompanying wooden pegs provided.

- **Dog Box™**. Dog learns to pick up blocks and insert them into the top of the box. Each time he succeeds a treat is discharged from box. The Dog Box comes with three different lid configurations to control the level of difficulty.

- **Dog Brick™**. Lets you hide the treats in the recesses located under a series of interlocking sliding blocks. Since the blocks can't be removed, your dog is required to locate the treats by sliding the blocks with either his paw or his nose in order to retrieve his reward.

- **Dog Smart™**. Hide a few treats in the recesses which are covered by hollow blocks. Your dog must locate the hidden treat by sense of smell. Since the blocks cannot be knocked over, your dog must lift the block with his teeth in order to retrieve the treat.

- **Dog Spinny™**. Hide a few treats in the recesses beneath the rotating top disc. Your dog must rotate the disc with its paw or nose in order to reveal and retrieve the treats.

- **Dog Tornado™**. This puzzle has four layers with rotating discs. Three of these layers have recesses

Our Cardigan Corgi, Lucy, adores solving puzzle toys. Here she works on the last layers of the Dog Tornado.

for concealing treats. Your dog is required to rotate the discs with his paw or nose in order to reveal and retrieve his reward.

- **Dog Trigger™**. Hide treats in each of the compartments behind the blocks. Place the Dog Trigger between your knees or on your lap at your dog's eye level. When your dog pushes the blocks with his nose the treat is discharged and dog receives his reward.

- **Dog Turbo™**. Insert treats into the restricted passages. Your dog is required to move the blocks toward the outside of the puzzle with his paw or nose in order to discharge the treat from the passage and collect his reward. You can vary the level of difficulty from easy to the more challenging mode.

For a simpler, homemade interactive toy, put treats inside cardboard boxes, food cartons, paper towel rolls, and tape them up securely, then let your dog shred them. The more vigorously your dog shreds, the more securely you can tape to give her more of a challenge.

Caution: Watch your dog so she doesn't ingest the cardboard or tape.

Of course, there are interactive toys that don't involve food. There are plush birdhouses that hide plush birds (with squeakers) for your dog to find, plush trees with squirrels, and beehives with bees. There's a plush Dachshund with rings that slide over the body for your dog to pull off. Egg Babies are stuffed toys with hidden eggs inside for your dog to find and remove—they come in Duck, Fish, Turtle, Dinosaur, and Hedgehog. Of course, unlike the balls and cubes, these toys require your participation (as do most good games!)—you have to put the birds back in the birdhouse, the bees back in the hive, the squirrels back in the tree, the rings back on the dog, and the eggs back in the babies, so your dog can play again.

Teaching Play Through Shaping

Playing with interactive toys teaches your dog that he can get good stuff by *doing* stuff—not just by sitting still and being a "good dog." This same concept is vital in the training game known as *shaping*—taking a behavior and breaking it down into small pieces, rewarding each piece until you build the complete behavior. Shaping teaches dogs to offer behavior rather than waiting to be told what to do. This is a trait valued by modern trainers, and sometimes scorned by old-fashioned trainers who tend to be more

Dubhy, our Scottish Terrier, is playing "101 Things to Do With a Foot Stool."

controlling in their training methods. Certainly a dog who feels comfortable offering behaviors can be a more inventive play partner!

If your dog hasn't yet learned the concept of offering behaviors, you can start with *free shaping*—you reinforce your dog for doing almost *anything*, until he realizes he can do lots of different things to get rewards. You'll want to use a *clicker* for this game (a small plastic box with a metal tongue that makes a "click!" sound when pressed)—or a special word, such as "Yes!" or "Tick!" that means he's earned a treat. This *reward marker* sound improves the timing of your reward—you can click the instant he does a rewardable behavior—you can't always get a treat to him instantly. The better your timing—the closer to the actual behavior he gets a reward or reward marker—the easier it is for your dog to figure out what the reward is for.

A very fun free shaping game is *101 Things To Do With A Box*. You can use any old cardboard box for this, or it doesn't even have to be a box, you can play "101 Things To Do With Anything." Your dog can be on leash, or off, if he'll stay with you. Set a chair a few feet back from the box or object, sit in the chair, and wait. You're looking for tiny pieces of behavior to click and treat—*any behavior* that relates to the box—a look, a step, a sniff, a push… You have no specific goal in mind, and you don't have to build up to a behavior—random behaviors are fine. If your dog seems hung up on one particular behavior you can stop clicking that one and wait for something else. The more confident your dog is about offering behaviors, the more easily you can just quit clicking one thing and wait for another. You want to click a lot, so look for even the tiniest of behaviors to click and reward. Remember that *every* time you click, your dog gets a treat.

Dubhy loves tricks. One of his favorites—playing the electronic keyboard, was accomplished through shaping.

Body parts shaping is good to help your dog learn to offer behavior, and it also helps you realize how precise this process can be for shaping the tiniest of movements. Sit in a chair with your dog facing you, and watch your dog closely for movement in one of his body parts. Even a tiny movement will do. For example, you could watch for a flick of his ear, a turn of his head, a lowering of his head, the lift of a paw, or a tongue flicker. When you have captured one of these movements with your click and treat, that's the one you'll continue to focus on. Sit and wait for another movement of that same body part. Click and treat. Your goal is to reinforce that accidental behavior until your dog begins deliberately offering it. When he does, you can name it, incorporate it into a trick routine, or keep working with it to shape it into something bigger if you choose.

Once you and your dog understand how shaping works, you can use it to teach all kinds of behaviors. In fact, it will make it much easier for your dog to figure out the more sophisticated interactive toys if he understands how to offer behaviors, and if you understand how to time your clicks perfectly—the *instant* he offers a rewardable behavior.

Value of Mind Games

Encourages your dog to think about what he needs to do to get you to reinforce him (to get good stuff). Teaches your dog to offer behaviors. The more behaviors your dog offers, the more behavior options you have to reinforce! A *must* for dogs who have to be on "restricted activity" due to medical or physical problems.

More Games

There are plenty more games you can play with your dog that don't fall into any particular category. If you haven't found the right game for you and your dog yet, or you just want more to add to his playlist, keep reading.

Arctic Freeze

Great game for a hot day… Fill a kiddy pool with several inches of water and dump several dozen ice cubes in it. Stand back and watch the fun!

Bowser Bowling

Think dogs can't bowl because they don't have opposable thumbs? Think again. Barbara Davis, positive trainer and Golden Retriever Rescuer from Corona, California plays several versions of Bowser Bowling with her dogs. This game takes some training.

First you have to teach your dog to nose-touch a medium sized, sturdy ball (Jolly Balls™ work) in your hand, gradually lowering the ball to the floor. This could take several sessions. Next, start reinforcing only for nose-touches that actually make the ball move. Now she understands that you want the ball to roll around. Finally, shape for the "bowling lane" concept by reinforcing touches that move the ball in a specific direction. You can create a bowling lane by using a wall on one side and a long rope on the other. Now you're ready to play.

Variation #1—Simple Bowling. Sit across from the dog (distance varies by breed, size, and skill level). Roll the ball to the dog. Dog must roll the ball back. *Expert Level*: Dog rolls the ball back on cue.

Variation #2—Lane Bowling. Set up a bowling lane using long leashes, ropes, tape, exercise pens— whatever you can use to mark the edges of a lane. The dog must repeatedly nudge the ball along the lane until it rolls across the finish line. *Expert Level*: Dog completes the lane with just one cue.

Variation #3—Competition Lane Bowling. Set up multiple lanes parallel to each other, one for each dog. Set one dog at the "top" of each lane with bowling ball in place. On cue everyone starts bowling; first one to cross the finish line wins.

You can make any of these variations even more challenging by purchasing a toddler's plastic bowling set and teaching the dog to actually roll the ball to knock down the pins. And keep score!

Bowser Basketball

Head back to the toddler's section of your local toy store for a Little Tykes™ basketball hoop and ball. You can teach your dog to drop the ball into the basket, or do what Shanna DeVries of Grandville, Michigan does with her Sheltie, Logan—she throws the ball to her dog so he can hit it into the basket with his nose.

Contact Sports

Some dogs enjoy and are stimulated by games that involve active physical contact. My husband plays Patty-Paws with Lucy, our Cardigan Corgi, when she's lying on the bed. He'll start patting at her paws and she'll swat back, eventually play-biting and getting vocal, and finally ending in a series of puppy-rushes around the bedroom.

Trainer and sculptress Michele Carra plays a version of Patty-Paws with her dog Annie while sitting in her wheelchair. She calls it "Hide the Feet." Michele describes the game as follows:

> With Annie sitting in front of me, I start covering her foot with mine. Of course she jerks it away, so then I cover her other foot. She gets silly and tries to grab my foot, but since I have two feet and she has one mouth it's hard for her to get me. Finally she gets smart and hides her feet under her chest and keeps swinging her mouth back and forth to protect them. Cute! Of course this one might backfire with the wrong dog…

Michele also uses her feet to play another contact game with Annie. "I have her lie down, and from my wheelchair I push her around with my feet," she says. "Annie loves it and lies on her back and wiggles around and moans. She's so fond of this game sometimes she'll block me on purpose so that I have to push her."

Thea, a tiny rescue Chihuahua, loves to play wrestle. Her owner, Andrea describes the game:

> If you have her up on the couch beside you and make bear claw hands at her, she bounces around and arrrooo arrroos at you, then paws at your hands. Not aggressive play on either of our parts, but interactive and enjoying—Thea's version of thumb wrestling, you'd think.

Caution: Contact Sports have the potential to encourage inappropriate biting and jumping. Avoid these games if you know your dog will become too aroused by this kind of activity. If you do play, stop the game if he gets too excited.

Trainer Lisa Waggoner's handsome Aussie, Gibson, plays King of the Fallen Log.

Jumping Games

Our family had Rough Collies (Lassies) as I was growing up, and I was the one who played with them the most. One of our favorite games was jumping. I would lay broomsticks and mop handles across chairs and cover them with towels and blankets to make jumps, and run through the house with our dogs, leaping over the jumps with them.

Trainer Mary Leatherberry plays one of our favorite games with her dog Angie: jumping on, over, or through things.

You can also play "Jump On Stuff." Positive trainer and good friend Lisa Waggoner of Murphy, North Carolina, plays "King of the Mountain" with Gibson, her Australian Shepherd. Lisa says,

> He's learned to jump up onto big logs or tree stumps, a chair in the classroom, or any object that's sturdy enough for him to safely jump on. It's so fun to watch him in the woods as he now offers the behavior when he comes to places where we've played the game before. He's my #1 playmate!

Kick the Pinecone

Positive trainer Tracey Schowalter of Gainesville, Georgia, says:

> When we're not playing "Chase the Tennis Ball," my Shepherd will find a pinecone (which we have plenty of) and carry it around. When I stop doing yard stuff, she'll lay the pinecone near my feet and back up a step or two. I'm supposed to try to kick it past her, which is very difficult. Sometimes I ask her to back up more, and sometimes I ask her to perform other behaviors before I kick it. Recently we added multiple pinecones to the game. It makes it easier to get one past her. I dance back and forth from one foot to the other (yes, my neighbors think I'm strange), and suddenly kick the pinecone with one of those moving feet. When she runs back with the pinecone in her mouth she's supposed to drop it before I'll kick the remaining one. So far she has brought me as many as four pine cones at one time.

> I recently discovered a wonderful thing. Playing "Kick the Pinecone" apparently trumps barking at

the UPS person. This is quite a revelation, as my Shepherd is a human-aggressive dog, and very reactive. Now if I hear the UPS truck pull into the driveway, all I have to do is say, 'Where's a pinecone, Eluki?' and she'll immediately go get a pinecone and become totally focused on me, waiting for me to kick it.

Talk to Your Dog

Some dogs make a lovely "roo-roo" sound and enjoy conversing with their owners. Encourage this conversation by giving your dog attention when she does it. You may be able to cue the behavior when you can tell she's "in the mood" by "roo-rooing" at her. You might even get her to sing with you!

Tricks

The line between tricks and games can blur very quickly. Positive trainers like to say "it's all tricks," since even the behaviors that we humans tend to consider "serious and important" are just behaviors we can get our dogs to do, reinforce, and put on cue. So it's all tricks, and in fact, if humans remembered to have as much fun teaching their dogs the "serious and important" behaviors as we do playing games and teaching tricks, no one would ever know the difference, and our dogs would think "Heel, sit, stay!" was as much fun as rolling over and jumping through hoops.

The tricks you can do with your dog are limited only by her physical capabilities and your imagination. If you need help in the creativity department, see the suggestions below, or find one of the many good books available on teaching your dog tricks.

Once you and your dog understand the positive rein-forcement training method, it becomes fairly easy to teach a wide range of new behaviors by using a food lure or the touch target to ask your dog to offer behaviors. Dogs are left or right-"pawed," so if circles don't work well in one direction, try the other direction. Remember: use the "Yes!" bridge word or Click! to encourage small attempts to per-form the behaviors (behavior shaping), and add the word *after* your dog is giving you the behavior. It is easiest to start with behaviors that are natural to your dog's personality and breed type. Be sure to be generous with your rewards!

This list describes just a few of the many things you can ask your dog to do:

1. **Take a Bow**. Offer a food lure (or touch target) at your dog's nose and move it slowly toward the floor to get the front end lowering while the hind end stays standing. You might get a full "Bravo" all at once, or you might have to shape it by click-ing (and rewarding) your dog for a slight lowering of the front while the rear stays elevated, gradually working up to a full bow.

2. **Roll Over**. Have your dog lie on his side, then use a lure or target to encourage her to roll on her back, then over. (Move the food slowly so she can follow it.)

3. **Crawl**. Have your dog lie down, then move the lure or target forward slowly, close to the ground, to get your dog to follow it without getting up.

4. **Weave**. Hold the lure or target between your legs and move it away from your dog to get him to walk between your legs. Take a step forward and have him walk under the other leg.

5. **"Bang!" (Play Dead).** Point your index finger at your dog with your thumb "cocked," say "Bang!" and ask your dog to relax flat on his side. Repetitions will make the connection between "Bang" and relax.

6. **Jump Over (or through) My Arm(s).** Kneel facing a wall, two feet away, with your dog on your left side. Touch the fingers of your left hand to the wall, arm low. Use the lure or target in your right hand to encourage your dog to jump over your arm. With your dog on your right side, switch arms and do it again.

7. **Spin/Twirl.** Move the lure or target in a slow circle at your dog's nose level, so your dog can follow. You can use different words for left and right hand circles.

8. **Circle Me.** Move the lure or target in a circle around you at your dog's nose level so he can follow.

9. **Reverse.** With your dog sitting or standing in front of you, gently step forward into your dog until he backs up. You may find it helpful to hold a treat in front of his nose. Not too high or he'll sit! You can practice next to a wall if he backs crooked.

10. **Side Pass.** With your dog standing in front of you, use a lure or target to keep her nose centered in front of you and slowly step sideways.

11. **Sit Nice (beg).** Hold the lure or target just above your dog's head. If he jumps up you are probably holding it too high. Reward small attempts to lift front paws off the ground at first.

12. **Dance**. Hold the lure or target the height of your dog's body length off the ground. When your dog stands on her hind legs, move the lure/target as if asking for a spin.

13. **Walk (on hind legs)**. Hold the lure/target the height of your dog's body length off the ground. When your dog stands, step backwards and encourage her to follow.

14. **Shake (Foot, "High Five")**. Close a food lure in your fist and hold it in front of your dog's nose. If he gets frustrated and paws at it to get it, "Yes!" and reward. If not, tickle or nudge a front foot until he lifts it. "Yes!" and reward. You can use a different word for each foot.

More Behaviors

Here are more behaviors to have fun with. You get to figure out how to get your dog to offer these to you!

1. Dry Off (Shake as if after a bath)

2. Figure 8 (Dog does figure 8 around your legs with you standing still)

3. Shake Head ("No" and "yes")

4. Play Possum (Lie on back with legs in air)

5. Lift a Hind Leg

6. Go 'Round (Send your dog around an object ahead of you)

7. Speak!

8. Whisper

9. Howl

10. Play the Piano

11. Count (Paw the ground)

12. Say Your Prayers

13. Salute

14. Shame (Hide your eyes)

15. Kiss

16. Hugs

17. Pups in a Blanket (Lie on blanket, grab one corner, roll over and cover yourself and sleep)

18. Moon-Walk (Back up while bowing)

19. Clean Up (Put toys in a basket or box)

20. Skate (Ride a skateboard)

21. Ding Dong (Ring bell with nose/Ring bell with paw/Ring bell by pulling string)

22. Sneeze

23. Wag Your Tail

24. What's Up? (Cock head to one side)

25. Step (Dog lifts leg when you lift yours)

Pat Miller's Favorite Group Games

I could go on almost forever sharing ideas for games you can enjoy with your dog, but we have to stop somewhere, so I'll end this chapter with some of my all-time favorite group games:

Musical Sits

We play this game (the easy version) in Week 4 of our Peaceable Paws Basic Good Manners Classes. It's always a big hit.

Easy. Have several dogs and humans in a large circle, all on leash. When the music starts, everyone starts walking in a circle (all the same direction, please!). When the music stops everyone gets their dog to sit (no pushing or pulling—verbal cues, hand signals and treat lures only!). First dog to sit gets a point; dog/human team with the most points at the end of the game wins.

Medium. Same as above version, except last dog to sit each time gets a "strike,"—three strikes and you're out. Winner is the last team to remain in the game.

Advanced. Same as above, except set out carpet squares around the circle, one less square than number of teams. When the music stops, each team must find a carpet square and dog must sit on square. Team without a square is eliminated. Winner is the last team to remain in the game.

Expert. Have two lines of chairs back-to-back in the center of the circle, one less chair than number of teams. Have carpet squares around the outside of the circle, same number of squares as number of dogs. When the music stops, human must have dog sit on a carpet square and *stay* while human runs and sits on chair. If dog gets up, human must *go back to dog* and have him sit again. Meanwhile, another human whose dog is still sitting on his square

may sit in the vacated chair. When all activity stops,
human without a chair is out (and so's her dog).

Musical Downs Variation

This is just a variation on Musical Sits—when the music stops, everyone has to get their dogs to lie down. All the
various levels apply.

Musical Behaviors Variation

With this game, instead of using music that stops to
cue humans to get their dog to do the behavior, the game
leader calls out a behavior such as sit, down, spin, rollover…
Whichever dog completes the behavior first gets a point;
dog-human team with the most points at the end of the
game wins. You can really get creative with this one—there
is an endless supply of various behaviors the game leader
could call for. Players might agree on a specified list of behaviors before starting, to make sure everyone at least has a
chance of performing them!

Red Light, Green Light

You might remember this one from grade school. You'll
need a fairly large space to play (depending on the number
of dogs in the group). Game leader stands on the far side
of the playing area with her back to the dog-human teams,
who are lined up side-by-side on the opposite side of the
playing field. When the game leader says "Green light!" all
of the teams start moving swiftly forward. Then the game
leader says "Red Light," pauses briefly and turns around. All
the teams stop and get their dogs to sit. No pushing, pulling, or jerking on dogs—they have to sit for a verbal cue,
a hand signal or a lure, or any combination of those three.
Anyone whose dog isn't sitting by the time the leader turns
around has to go back to the starting line. The winner is the
team that reaches the leader first.

Treats in Spoons

Players stand in a large circle with their dogs, game leader in the middle of the circle. Each human player holds a treat-filled teaspoon in the same hand as she's holding her dog's leash. When leader says "Forward!," all players begin walking in the same direction around the circle. If any treats fall from the spoon, that player and her dog are out. The winner is the last team with no dropped treats. If several players are very adept at keeping teats on their spoons, the leader can call for teams to run, stop suddenly, lie down, spin—the sky's the limit…

No fair using peanut butter or squeeze cheese!

Bobbing for Dogs

Our wonderful Pomeranian, Dusty, absolutely adored playing this game. In fact, he'd get so excited when he saw us setting it up, he'd shake all over and couldn't wait for his turn to bob for dogs.

Put room-temperature water in a cooking pot or stainless steel bowl—a few inches for small dogs, more for large dogs. Slice a hotdog into pennies one-eighth to one-quarter-inch thick. Drop them in the water and tell your dog to get them. You can even set this one up at a competition—the dog who eats all his hotdog pieces first wins. Be sure to get hotdogs that sink to the bottom of the pan for even more entertainment value!

Now, go play with your dog!

CHAPTER 6
THE FAMILY THAT PLAYS TOGETHER, STAYS TOGETHER
CHILDREN AND DOGS

Everyone in the family, including children, should play with their dogs. Even young children can be suitable playmates for many dogs, with some important caveats. Assuming your dog likes to play, the more humans she gets to play with, the more humans she'll think are wonderful because they make good stuff happen, and the better socialized she'll be. Dogs who are well-socialized are far less likely to bite or otherwise engage in behaviors that are likely to get them into serious trouble.

In addition, the more that each family member has fun interacting with the dog, the more likely it is that the dog will stay in that home for her entire life. As I've said since page one of this book, play helps build strong bonds, and relationships that support lifelong loving homes for canine family members.

However, that doesn't mean that all play activities are appropriate for all family members. Children and seniors are most at risk for injury from inappropriate dog behavior, because they are generally the most fragile and vulnerable of our human family members. In the first eleven months of 2007, there were 30 dog-related fatalities in the U.S. Of these, fifteen of the victims were children age ten years or younger, and nine were adults over the age of 60. A few years ago a young child was tragically killed by a wonderful Golden Retriever who saw the flapping ends of the child's scarf as an invitation to play Tug. There was no adult present to intervene, and the child was strangled. The dog was rehomed.

Dogs Playing With Children

It is imperative that parents observe some important caveats about allowing their children to play with dogs. It's also imperative that parents and dog owners have a very clear understanding of dog body language in order to allow their children to play *safely* with dogs. In order to be a good candidate for child play, a dog should absolutely *love* children. He approaches them eagerly and with a happy expression, tail waving at half mast, body loose and relaxed. Given the choice, he'd rather be with kids than with the old folks. He's delighted to baby-sit, and looks crestfallen when the children leave him behind. His idea of heaven is having a toddler tug on his ears. Anything less than all-out enthusiasm for children is merely canine *tolerance* for little humans. A dog who only tolerates the presence of children is at risk for biting when he's pushed beyond his tolerance limits.

Here are the child-play caveats:

1. Interactions (not just play) between young children and dogs should always be closely supervised by an adult, whether the children are visitors or family members. Things don't have to go as tragically wrong as a dog-related fatality for a child to be injured and the blame placed on the dog. Dogs who

These puppies are getting a good dose of child-socialization thanks to this gentle young man who is playing very appropriately with them. Interactions between young children and dogs should always be closely supervised.

Children should only interact with dogs who clearly enjoy children.

Goldendoodle Spotty is enjoying winter sports with his family.

hurt children often lose their homes, whether the dog was justified in biting or not. The definition of "young child" varies depending on the size, personality and activity level of the dog, but a child under 6-8 years old definitely qualifies, and sometimes older.

2. Games between dogs and children should be restricted to those activities that don't encourage high arousal or nipping/biting behaviors.

3. Children should only interact/play with dogs who clearly enjoy children. Dogs who only *tolerate* children can too easily be pushed over their threshold for tolerance by normal child behavior. Dogs who adore children will forgive normal-but-annoying small human activities. Dogs who tolerate or dislike children should be managed to prevent their access to children. If children are a regular presence in their lives, they should be enrolled in a program to modify their behavior and help them learn to enjoy the presence of children.

Dogs who are going to play with children should adore, not just tolerate, small humans. This dog looks a little stressed about being in school, but it could be he's just not accustomed to sitting at a desk—or the teacher just announced a pop quiz!

Border Collie Flip, pulls "his" child, Monica, on a saucer. Flip has been well-trained, and the pair are closely supervised by mom/dog trainer Stacey Braslau-Schneck.

4. The most appropriate dog/child games are those that direct the dog's energy (and teeth and paws) toward objects *other* than the human.

5. Many dogs have predictable cycles of activity—times in the day when they seem to have more energy, times when they have less. For some dogs—especially high-energy ones, the lower energy periods of the activity cycle are more appropriate times to schedule play sessions with children. Alternatively, an adult can engage in energy-draining activities with the dog first, and invite the child to play with the dog when he (the dog) is tired.

6. Children *must* be taught appropriate, gentle behavior with dogs. Training and play should both come from a foundation of positive training. If adults model inappropriate behavior, children will copy

Tired dogs—and tired kids—are more likely to be well-behaved; demonstrated here by Scott Bentley and his dog Sean.

it. Under no circumstances should children be al-
lowed/encouraged to verbally or physically coerce,
intimidate, or punish dogs. Children who are de-
sensitized to the pain of animals may also desen-
sitize to the pain of other humans. It's never too
early in a child's development to begin teaching
empathy and kindness.

Dogs cannot learn that it's okay to nip at some children
sometimes, and not other times. Hence the importance of
total supervision with dogs and kids—if a dog learns the fun
game of chasing and nipping at running, screaming children, he's likely to see all little humans as running, screaming play partners. While one child may enjoy arousing a dog
by running and screaming in play, another child may be
truly frightened, running from an apparently aggressive dog
in true fear or panic.

I recommend the following as appropriate play activities
for *most* child-friendly dogs and children (discussed in detail
in Chapter 4). There are, of course, always exceptions. And
remember, these are still *supervised* play activities. Always.

Find It

Find a hidden treat, find a hidden object, find hidden treats in a tub, are all great dog-kid games. If your dog
guards resources (gets tense, growly, or even bites, when in
proximity to or possession of valuable objects) then the child
needs to be (and stay) a safe distance from the hiding place
when the dog is sent to "Find it!" Children love being the
hidden person in "Find the person" games—although their
giggling often gives away their hiding place. "Finding a treat
in the hand" may or may not be appropriate for children. If
the dog is very soft and gentle when indicating which hand
holds the treat, this is fine. If the dog uses teeth or any real
level of intensity to indicate the treat-hand, then not.

Running

Supervised running can be acceptable providing the dog is self-controlled when running—that is, she will run politely with the child without jumping up and/or nipping. These dogs are probably the exception, rather than the rule.

The herding breeds are notoriously inappropriate for child-running games, as their natural herding instincts often compel them to jump and nip. It's unfair (and usually ineffective!) to punish your Border Collie for chasing after and nipping at running children. This is akin to punishing your Labrador Retriever for bringing back a tennis ball. They are genetically programmed to respond with predictable behaviors to certain stimuli. Herding dogs are programmed to chase things that move, try to stop the movement, and herd them back. This is a situation where management is called for—when children want to run and play, Missy should be put away.

Of course, there are always exceptions. There are herding dogs who won't chase and nip. If you have one of those, management isn't needed around running children. Supervision still is.

Running games that don't involve humans running are more appropriate for children. "Monkey in the Middle" is an excellent choice for kid participation. "Red Light/Green Light" can be a good compromise, since it involves only short stretches of running, with the dog demonstrating self-control with the required "sit" behavior each time the team halts.

Chasing

I don't recommend "Tag" and "Gimme" type games for children, as the cues and rules can be too confusing for them to be able to use and follow. Kids can play "Round

The most appropriate dog/child games are those that direct the dog's energy toward objects other than the small human.

Robin Recall," as long as the dog isn't a jumper/nipper. Play that involves chasing *stuff* can be excellent dog/kid games. My first Australian Kelpie, Keli, could keep a young child entertained for hours with her obsession for chasing tennis balls. The caveat here is that the dog must be polite about giving back the object being thrown. "Blowing bubbles" is a great kid choice—they tend to like bubbles anyway, and they don't have to worry about getting the dog to give bubbles back, they just make more! Chasing water from the end of the hose is another good activity for dog/kid play—the water—and the dog—are far from the child and not likely to inflict any damage.

Digging

This activity *can* be appropriate play for children and dogs, providing the canine digger is not too intense about his digging, doesn't resource guard, and shows reasonable regard for the presence of human body parts.

Tug

I do not recommend "Tug" for young children. The rules are too complicated, and the level of canine arousal too high for safe dog-child interaction.

Mind Games

Many of the interactive mind-game activities are either self-play (dog pushes Buster Cube™ around to make food fall out) or somewhat complicated—requiring good observation skills, decision-making, and timing to help the dog succeed in performing the designated behaviors. Most of these are probably too complex for young children, but older children can excel at playing these kind of games with dogs once they understand the concepts.

A Few More

By now, you should have an understanding of the guidelines I use to determine what kind of play is appropriate for children. I just want to point out a few more (below) that are ideal dog-kid activities. Remember that interactions (not just play) between young children and dogs should *always* be supervised. I can never say that often enough.

The "Freeze" part of "Go Wild and Freeze" should be taught to every child who interacts with your dog, after your dog is reliable with the "freeze" response. "Arctic Freeze"— ice cubes in a kiddie pool—can be fun for kids and dogs both on a hot day. "Simple Bowling" is another perfect kid-entertainer. Children are often enchanted by a dog who will roll the ball back to them, and your Bowling Bowser can baby-sit for hours (with your supervision!). Many of the "Group Games" are suitable for or can be adapted for children. And kids love to teach dogs to do "Tricks." Be creative...and supervise!

Dogs Playing With Adults

Adults can have a lot more latitude in their dog-play activities. Generally more able to withstand aroused dog behavior, and more able to understand and play by the rules, grown-up humans can select appropriate games from a much wider range of choices. There are still some caveats, however, even with adult play.

Some adults won't play by the rules. It's up to you to lay down the law. "Tug" may be off-limits to an adult friend who allows or encourages your dog to put teeth on clothing or skin. *All* play may be off-limits to an adult who becomes abusive in his interactions with your dogs. In my world, either that person wouldn't come to my house, or my dogs would be put away when he's here—he wouldn't even be allowed to see or touch them.

Senior adults, mentioned previously, also need to be protected from over-aroused dog play. Make wise decisions about these interactions as well. Restrict play choices to safe, calm activities that won't risk injury to a fragile adult, or one who may not be steady on her feet. Lots of older adults also enjoy teaching dogs to perform gentle tricks.

Always remember that each dog—and each human—is an individual. Play activities that are offered here as appropriate for dog/child/adult play may *not* be appropriate for your particular dog, or child, or the adults who want to play with your dog. Ultimately the safety of your dog and the humans who interact with her is your responsibility, regardless of what any book, friend, trainer, or other dog-care professional tells you.

Chapter 7
DON'T PLAY IN TRAFFIC
HOW NOT TO PLAY WITH YOUR DOG

Since positive trainers focus on what *to* do far more than what *not* to do, this chapter on "how not to play with your dog" will be relatively brief. There are just a few cautions I'd like you to keep in mind as you go about playing with your canine pal. These "don'ts" are designed to keep you and your family members (canine *and* human) safe, as well as visitors to your home, and those you may meet out in public.

Reinforce Inappropriate Behaviors (Don't!)

All animals repeat behaviors that are reinforcing (rewarding) to them. Behaviors that aren't reinforced decrease, and eventually go away. Unwelcome behaviors that can be inadvertently reinforced during play include:

- Biting/Nipping
- Barking
- Jumping up
- Grabbing things out of your hands
- Running away

Of course, some of the above may be included as part of the game: you *can* incorporate barking, jumping up, and running away as part of the fun if you choose to do so. If so, you'll be wise to put those behaviors on cue, use a cue that won't easily be mistaken for something a guest might do, and take the time to teach your dog she *only* gets reinforced for those behaviors if/when you give her the cue (permission) to do them.

Perhaps you decide you want jumping up to be part of your playing fun. I taught my Terrier mix, Josie, that she could jump up and put her paws on me (hug) if I knelt down and patted the tops of my shoulders. Not likely that some random visitor would do that—and if they did, then Josie was free to hug them as well.

"Running away" (dog running away from you) was discussed at length as a game in Chapter 5. If you choose to reinforce this behavior as part of play, be sure to use a cue to initiate the game, pause occasionally to call your dog to you during the game (with a *big* reward when he comes), and don't fall into the trap of accepting your dog's invitation to play "keep away" when you haven't asked for it—or you risk not being able to catch her when you really need to.

Biting, nipping, and grabbing things from your hands are behaviors that are better *never* being reinforced. In some communities, it only takes one over-aroused nip to a child to put your dog on your local "dangerous dog" list with a requisite period of quarantine. At best, it's a temporary inconvenience, and your dog now has a "record" at Animal Control. At worst, it can be the first step to a very unhappy ending.

If your dog offers these unwanted behaviors during play, you can try time-outs: "Oops! Time-out!" Nipping makes all of the fun stop! Your cheerful "Oops!" should be uttered at the exact moment the undesirable behavior occurs, to let your dog know what he did to make the game stop. This is the opposite of the clicker or other reward marker, which tells the dog the instant he's earned a reward. The actual time-out is a brief period of social deprivation; you can remove your dog from the room, or leave him in the room and remove yourself. If some of the games you play with your dog seem to encourage these inappropriate behaviors despite your consistent and timely use of time-outs, you might be wise to make different play choices.

Model Inappropriate Behaviors (Don't!)

Adults, as well as the children around you, will mimic your behavior with your dog—how you play with her, how you train. "Do as I say, not as I do," is rarely an effective way to positively influence the behavior of others. If you want others to play gently with your dog, don't let them see you being rough with her. If you want them to follow the rules for Tug, or Chase games, you'd best follow them yourself. If you want them to treat her with respect, be respectful yourself in your relationship with your canine best friend.

Flip-Flop (Don't!)

Dogs simply can't understand the concept of "Just this once," or "Only on special occasions." You need to be consistent with whatever rules you set in place for playtime. That doesn't mean you can never be spontaneous with your dog—what fun is play without spontaneity? However, if your house rules include "No play in the kitchen," stick to your guns—or be prepared to have Dasher spontaneously romping under your feet as you carry that pan of boiling spaghetti water to the sink to drain.

Don't Flip-Flop! If you're not going to allow your dog to play on the sofa (the Miller dogs are allowed), don't do it even once!

Overwhelm Your Dog (Don't!)

Some peoples' idea of dog-play seems to be limited to physical roughhousing. It amazes me that time and again, I see a person's first attempt to play with an unfamiliar dog start at "roughhouse." When the dog is unwilling to participate, the human either persists at tormenting the dog, confident that he'll play eventually (he won't), or tones it down a little at a time to try to accommodate the dog. By then, however, the dog's so intimidated by the wild and crazy human that he's not the least bit interested in any kind of play, thank you very much.

If you've read this far in the book, hopefully you realize there are lots of different ways to play with your dog, some of them very thoughtful and gentle. While some dogs do enjoy rough-and-tumble games, others are quite put off by them. Like lovemaking, you need to understand and be able

This shelter dog is overwhelmed by the assessor's attempt to play. Note the dog's lowered body carriage, tucked tail, and turned head.

to adapt your style of play to your partner's preferences if you want to ensure an enjoyable experience for both parties. You probably have a good idea already of your own dog's play preferences. If you're meeting a new dog, start with the small stuff, and take your cues from him—increasing the arousal and physicality of your play at the dog's invitation as you explore games he may already know, and teach him new ones.

As you play, be sure to observe his body language for subtle signs that he's not having a good time. Failure to make eye contact, flattened ears, lowered body posture, subdued demeanor, or a polite disinclination to repeat the play, are all signs that your dog's not as comfortable with the game as you may think. For more information on understanding canine body language, read *Canine Body Language: A Photographic Guide* by Brenda Aloff, and/or watch *The Language of Dogs:*

*Understanding Canine Body Language and Other Communi-
cation Signals,* an excellent DVD set by Sarah Kalnajs.

There are, of course, those sad dogs who never learned
how to play with humans. If you find yourself with one of
those, Chapter 8 should prove useful to you.

Chapter 8

LET US PLAY

REHABILITATING THE PLAY-DEPRIVED DOG

For a dog, playing with humans is a learned behavior. Dogs who don't have the opportunity to play with humans early in life may grow up with a play behavior deficit—one that can interfere with their ability to connect with the two-legged members of their family in a way that's important and meaningful.

The wise breeder makes sure she plays creatively with her pups, and invites others to play with them as well, so the dogs grow up to be comfortable playing all kinds of games with all kinds of different humans. Pups raised around children tend to know how to play with humans, as kids are natural players. Children don't always know to follow the rules of good dog-play, but they do play!

Unfortunately, a significant number of dogs grow up play-deprived. These may be dogs from puppy mills who spent the first formative months of their lives in cages at the mill, and then at the pet store. They may be dogs who were "kennel-raised" by a breeder, with minimal play interaction with humans. They might even be dogs who were purchased as pups by humans with good intentions, but who ended up in the backyard, or in the home of one or more play-deprived humans who just didn't understand the importance of frolicking with Fido. I couldn't find any kind of estimate on how many dogs don't know how to do people-play, but if the dogs we see at the shelter are any measure, there are a lot of them out there.

With play-deprived dogs, it's extremely important that you not use verbal or physical corrections in your training program. In order to be willing to let his guard down to play, your dog needs to know he can trust you to not hurt him. Dogs trained with positive methods learn that it's safe to offer new behaviors—and that's exactly what play will be for your play-challenged dog—a new behavior. Dogs trained with punishment or corrections often learn that the safest thing to do is…nothing. A dog who is already inhibited about play will be quite content to do nothing, and never engage in play, *especially* when he knows you could turn violent if he makes a wrong move.

If you're having trouble convincing your dog to play with you, you may need to change your approach to dog-play, you may need to teach him to play, or you may need a combination of the two. Here are some mistakes commonly made by people trying to convince a reluctant dog to play:

- Too much intensity, and the pressure turns the dog off the game.

- Shoving a toy at the dog, pushing it into his face to try to get him to play with it.

- Getting too excited when the dog is just starting to show interest in playing, and frightening the dog as a result.

- Expecting the dog to play one particular game, such as "Fetch," without exploring other possibilities.

Continued on page 126.

In this series of three photos, this shelter worker is gently attempting to get this dog to play with a toy during the assessment process. And she succeeds! First the dog starts to show some interest. Eventually he overcomes his stress and engages in a retrieve game.

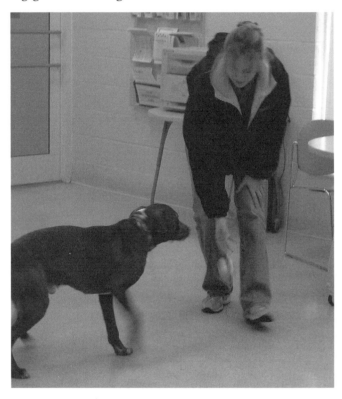

- Giving up on the dog.

- Failing to recognize and reinforce embryonic play behaviors.

- Relying on food only as a reinforcer to teach play.

- "Lumping" rather than "splitting"—expecting full-fledged play rather than taking small play efforts and very gradually shaping them into play.

- Getting "stuck" with small play efforts, and not helping the dog build them into bigger games.

- Not ending sessions soon enough—keep them short and sweet; leave the dog wanting more!

Teaching Play

There are a number of different techniques you can use to get your dog interested in and comfortable with dog-human play. Make note of any time when your dog seems particularly cheerful or lighthearted—these can give you clues as to how he might best be prompted to play. Food can often encourage a dog to play, since all dogs eat—or they starve to death…

You can experiment with the play-training techniques described below, and see which ones start to capture your dog's interest. Remember, *go slow*, and control your own excitement level. Some dogs are turned off to play because the human starts acting really bizarre as soon as the dog loosens up a little. Rein in your own impulse to celebrate your dog's first small play efforts so you don't accidentally intimidate him. If he perceives your excitement as aversive, you will actually be punishing him for trying to play, and are likely to shut down his embryonic play behavior.

As you experiment, remember to watch for, appreciate, treasure, and gently reinforce even the tiniest bits of play behavior. These might include:

- A flip of the head

- A flirty sideways glance

- A quick bounce

- A sudden paw movement

- A brief lowering of the head, chest and shoulders

- A short step forward, sideways or back

- A dip of the head

- A bark

Make a note of what you—or the environment—might have done to elicit that behavior, and try to recreate it. Be casual—if you're too obvious or deliberate, your reluctant canine player may shut down.

Create Desire

Dawn Mellon, Certified Pet Dog Trainer in Talent, Oregon, teaches Agility, and finds she often has to teach people how to teach their dogs to play, play being an important reinforcer for successful Agility dogs. She claims the following program never fails:

- Slice open a stuffed toy and pull some of the stuffing out, or purchase a "food toy" with a Velcro opening, designed for this purpose. Place the toy somewhere that the dog can see it, but not reach it. Several times a day, go to the toy and play with it—tossing it in the air; letting it fall to the floor and "grabbing" it; letting your dog watch you put treats in it.

• When your dog is starting to show interest in the toy and your activities, create *interaction*. (It works best to do this when he's somewhat hungry.) Sit on the floor and let your dog see you stuff the toy with treats. Toss and catch it a couple of times, then let it fall, or drag it around the floor.

• If your dog approaches the toy at all, open up the toy and let him eat all the treats, telling him what a good boy he is.

• Repeat two more times, then put the toy away, out of reach, but where he can see it. You can even feed your dog all his meals this way for a week or so.

Interest is what it's all about. Lucy, our Corgi, shows intense interest in her expression as she waits for someone to kick her Genius toy.

- Gradually be slower and slower to "help" your dog by opening the toy. You should see your dog begin to take more initiative himself—perhaps touching the toy with his nose or paw, eventually picking the toy up in his mouth or trying to rip it open to get the treats. Continue to open the toy for him as he becomes more motivated to interact with it, until he's enthusiastically interacting with it.

Find It

The "Find It" game, discussed at length in Chapter 5, also capitalizes on your dog's natural desire to eat food—especially high-value treats. As you toss treats back-and-forth in Step 1 of the game, watch for small signs that he's loosening up and enjoying himself. Toss a couple more treats and then stop—remember to end when he's enjoying the activity, and don't overwhelm him with your enthusiasm.

You might even start the game when you're not really thinking about play, but perhaps just sitting on the sofa watching television. Toss a few treats from time to time, and don't worry if your dog thinks of it as play. When you start to see a little eager anticipation in his eyes as he waits for the next toss, you know you're on the right track.

Physical Play

A dog who is intimidated by or simply not interested in playing with a toy, may be more amenable to body contact play. Touch very gently and playfully at first, building to more active contact games over numerous sessions (weeks, maybe months!) as he warms to the game concept. Experiment with touch on different parts of his body to see what might elicit a tiny play response. Some dogs get excited if you softly touch a paw, an ear, a nose, a belly—just watch

that you don't use too much energy and frighten your dog
with your touch.

Shaping Play

Shaping lends itself perfectly to teaching remedial play
skills. The very definition of shaping—breaking a behavior
into tiny pieces and reinforcing the pieces until you build
the complete behavior—is exactly what's needed for many
play-deprived or play-reluctant dogs. Revisit the section on
shaping in Chapter 5, especially the "101 Things to Do
With a Box" game, and use a toy or other play object in
place of the box.

Remember that you need to look for the tiniest pieces
of behavior to click and treat so your dog wins a lot and can
enjoy success. Even if it doesn't look like play to you, the
more you get your dog to freely and happily offer behavior,
the sooner the behavior will start to look like play.

Capturing Play

All but the most unsocialized, fearful dogs will occasionally offer some spontaneous play behavior, even if ever-
so-briefly. If you have conditioned your dog to a reward
marker—the clicker, or a verbal "Yes," "Click," "Tick," or
whatever marker you chose, you can teach your dog to play
by capturing and rewarding those spontaneous moments.

Watch your dog for the tiniest of play behaviors—a
quick bounce, a flip of the head, a sideways flirt. The instant
you see anything that even vaguely resembles spontaneous
play, click your clicker or utter your verbal marker and toss
your dog a high-value treat. You can praise gently—remember not to overwhelm your dog! Because all living creatures
repeat behaviors that are rewarding to them, when your dog
realizes she's getting clicked and treated for play behaviors,

she will offer them more frequently, and, over time, with increased enthusiasm. Before you know it, your dog will be playing with you for the sheer joy of play.

Now that you're armed with all kinds of ideas for the whole continuum of canine playmates, go play with your dog!

Thanks!

I want to thank the following dog-lovers who contributed a wealth of play ideas for Chapter 5 and various other parts of this book. These are clearly humans who know how to play, and their dogs are lucky to have them!

Elizabeth Adamec
Windsor Mill, Maryland
www.sweetwag.com
sweetwag@gmail.com
(410) 493-8027
    Sweet Wag is a complete training service, serving the Greater Baltimore/Washington area including Annapolis and surrounding areas. We provide group classes as well as private in-home instruction using all positive methods.

Irith Bloom
Los Angeles, California

Michele Carra
Doggone Leash!
Winchester, Virginia

Gina Crimmins
Bartlett, Illinois
(847) 274-1878
    Family and dog friendly group and private lessons

Frances Dauster, CPDT
P's & Q's Dog Training! LLC
Grand Bay, Alabama
www.sunpaws.com
dobemom@juno.com
(251) 786-7297
    Gentle training, small classes! In home Behavioral Consultations and individual instruction. Puppy, Manners, Obedience classes! Kennel-free home-style boarding, Doggy Day Care, and lots more!

Barbara Davis, CPDT, CDBC
BADDogsInc LLC
Corona, California
barbara@baddogsinc.com
www.baddogsinc.com
866-LUV-A-DOG
    Positive dog training and behavior consulting services for the family dog, incorporating only gentle techniques designed to enhance the loving relationship between dogs and their people.

Paula Denby-Gibbs
Melbourne, Victoria, Australia
pjdg@positives4pets.com
www.positives4pets.com
    Pet training services—classes, workshops, fun days, behaviour consultations and individual consultations.

Shanna Devries
Grandville, Michigan

Laura Dorfman, CPDT
Glencoe, Illinois
Kona's Touch, Inc. "Gentle teachings for you & your dog"
www.konastouch.com
Positive, peaceful, in-home private lessons, consultation, puppy and dog training, good manners and behavior issues. Holistic health and nutrition options.

Kristina N. Gage, CPDT
SmartDog Dog Training
Saratoga Springs, NY
training@smartdogschool.com
www.smartdogschool.com
(518) 893-7444
Family dog training (group classes or private lessons), Rally, and behavioral consultations. In and around Saratoga Springs.

Sandra Garcia-Pelayo
Seattle, Washington
Buena Vista Dog Training
Buenavistadoggtraining@yahoo.com
(206) 234-7583
Private Training for puppies and adult dogs. Basic manners, obedience, and behavioral problems. Fun, effective methods based on animal learning theory.

Debbie Gary-Taskey
BeeHaven Caine Coaching
Friedens, Pennsylvania
dgtbee@yahoo.com
(814) 445-6036
Basic Manners, Basic Agility, Pet First Aid/CPR.

Beverly Hebert
Houston, Texas

Bonnie Hess, BA, ABCDT
Faithful Companion Dog Training, LLC
Lancaster, Pennsylvania
www.faithfulcompanion.com
Bonnie@faithful-companion.com
   I offer puppy socialization and manners classes, dog group classes, and private training using a positive, gentle approach.

Jessica Jankowski
Goffstown, New Hampshire
www.puppyplease.com
Jessica@puppyplease.com
(603) 261-9283
   Positive training for the pet dog, puppies to adults. Careful, thoughtful customized training to develop the best relationship between families and pets.

Susan Kaminsky
The Country Dog
Darien, Connecticut
susandk@optonline.net
(203) 434-2884

C. Chelsea Koslow
Saratoga Springs, NY
Paws-for-praise@hotmail.com
   Reward-based puppy manners/socialization and beginner through advanced lessons, all focused on effective communication and building a positive, loving relationship.

Jules Lockwood Nye, CPDT
Severn, Maryland
Sit Stay & Play
www.sitstayandplay.com
info@sitstayandplay.com
    Group Classes, Private Lessons (our place or yours), Puppy Socialization, Doggie Daycare, Cat Training, Specializing in training for deaf and blind dogs.

Doug Lowing
Amherst, Massachusetts
delowing@gmail.com

Jean Mammen
Washington, DC

Dawn Mellon, CPDT
Talent, Oregon
dawn@cooperativecanines.net
www.cooperativecanines.net
    Group and private lessons for Agility, Obedience, Rally, and Pet Manners. Behavior consultations. Relationship counseling for performance dog handlers.

Lisa Phagan
Anderson, Indiana

Tracey Schowalter
Puppy Adept, Inc.
Gainesville, Georgia
info@puppyadept.com
www.puppyadept.com
(770) 967-7836
    Behavior modification and group and private training for dogs of all ages.

Julie Sontag, CTC, CPDT
One Smart Puppy, Inc.
New York, New York
www.one-smart-puppy.com

Laura Van Dyne, CPDT
The Canine Consultant LLC
Carbondale, Colorado
(970) 96303745
Group and private classes using positive reinforcement, management and realistic expectations.

Lisa Waggoner
Cold Nose College
Murphy, North Carolina
www.ColdNoseCollege.com
lisa@coldnosecollege.com
(828) 644-9148
Specializing in effective, reward-based clicker training for the family dog to help them become well-behaved companions and family members. We offer in-home training, small group classes and behavior modification within the Tri-state area of North Carolina, Georgia, and Tennessee.

Marilyn Wolf, BS, CPDT
New Port Richey, Florida
marilyn@KorrectKritters.com
www.KorrectKritters.com
(727) 372-9825
In-home training only; I specialize in working with family pets to improve or repair relationships so all can live together more comfortably.

RECOMMENDED READING

Beyond Fetch. Fun, Interactive Activities for You and Your Dog. D. Caroline Coile, Ph.D.

Canine Body Language. A Photographic Guide. Brenda Aloff

The Dog Whisperer. Paul Owens

Dogs Never Lie About Love. Jeffery Moussaieff Masson

For the Love of a Dog. Patricia McConnell, Ph.D.

How Dogs Learn. Mary Bailey and John Burch

How to Speak Dog, Stanley Cohen

The Language of Dogs. Understanding Canine Body Language and Other Communication Signals, DVD set. Sarah Kalnajs

Living With Kids and Dogs Without Losing Your Mind. Colleen Pelar

Off-Leash Dog Play. Robin Bennett and Susan Briggs

The Other End of the Leash. Patricia McConnell

Positive Perspectives. Love Your Dog, Train Your Dog. Pat Miller

Positive Perspectives 2. Know Your Dog, Train Your Dog. Pat Miller

The Power of Positive Dog Training, 2nd edition. Pat Miller

ABOUT THE AUTHOR

Pat B. Miller is at the forefront of the force-free, positive dog training phenomenon in the United States. She is a Past President of APDT, the world's largest professional group of dog trainers, operates her own training facility in Hagerstown, Maryland, and is a 20-year veteran of humane work. Pat is a popular columnist for *Whole Dog Journal*, *Your Dog*, and *Popular Dogs* and is the author of *Positive Perspectives. Love Your Dog, Train Your Dog; Positive Perspectives 2. Know Your Dog, Train Your Dog;* and *The Power of Positive Dog Training.* Pat's five dogs are rescues of various breeds and sizes.

INDEX

PHOTOS BY

Louis B. Ruediger: Cover
Chris Danker: 9, 34a, 107a
Marvin L. Smith: 10, 18, 31a, 32,
Charles W. Fellers, Jr.: 13, 59
Laura Dorfman: 16, 27a, 29, 52, 55
Melissa L. Ordway: 19
Susan Hughs: 20, 22
William Buzzell: 21, 60
Susan Hughes: 22
Pat Miller: 27, 31a, 33b, 39, 49, 53, 56, 72, 81, 83, 86, 88, 90,
    119, 120, 124a, 124b, 125, 128
Shirley Bennett: 33a,
Lori Shemik: 34a
Brian Ervin: 48a and b
Lisa Waggoner: 94
Jim Leatherberry: 95
CJ Bentley: 107, 110, 114
Joey Thorne: 108
Brad Stanley, courtesy of Michigan Humane Society: 109a
Stacy Braslau-Schneck: 109b

From Dogwise Publishing
www.dogwise.com, 1-800-776-2665

BEHAVIOR & TRAINING
ABC's of Behavior Shaping, DVD. Ted Turner
Aggression In Dogs. Brenda Aloff
Am I Safe? DVD. Sarah Kalnajs
Behavior Problems in Dogs, 3rd ed. William Campbell
Brenda Aloff's Fundamentals, DVD. Brenda Aloff
Bringing Light to Shadow. Pam Dennison
Canine Body Language. Brenda Aloff
Clicked Retriever. Lana Mitchell
Dog Behavior Problems. William Campbell
Dog Detectives. Kat Albrecht
Dog Friendly Gardens. Cheryl Smith
Dog Language. Roger Abrantes
Ethical Dog Trainer. Jim Barry
Evolution of Canine Social Behavior, 2nd ed. Roger Abrantes
Fighting Dominance in a Dog Whispering World, DVD. Jean Donaldson and Ian Dunbar
Focus Not Fear. Ali Brown
Give Them a Scalpel and They Will Dissect a Kiss, DVD. Ian Dunbar
Guide To Professional Dog Walking And Home Boarding. Dianne Eibner
How To Run A Dog Business. Veronica Boutelle
Language of Dogs, DVD. Sarah Kalnajs
Mastering Variable Surface Tracking, Component Tracking (2 bk set). Ed Presnall
Mindful Dog Teaching. Claudeen McAuliffe
My Dog Pulls. Turid Rugaas
New Knowledge of Dog Behavior (reprint). Clarence Pfaffenberger
Oh Behave! Jean Donaldson
On Talking Terms with Dogs, 2nd edition. Turid Rugaas

On Talking Terms with Dogs, DVD. Turid Rugaas
Positive Perspectives. Pat Miller
Positive Perspectives 2. Pat Miller
Positive Training for Show Dogs. Vicki Ronchette
Predation and Family Dogs, DVD. Jean Donaldson
Really Reliable Recall, DVD. Leslie Nelson
Right on Target. Mandy Book & Cheryl Smith
Stress in Dogs. Martina Scholz & Clarissa von Reinhardt
The Dog Trainer's Resource. Mychelle Blake (*ed*)
Therapy Dogs. Kathy Diamond Davis
Training Dogs, A Manual (reprint). Konrad Most
Training the Disaster Search Dog. Shirley Hammond
Try Tracking. Carolyn Krause
Visiting the Dog Park. Cheryl S. Smith
When Pigs Fly. Jane Killion
Winning Team. Gail Haynes
Working Dogs (reprint). Elliot Humphrey & Lucien Warner

HEALTH & ANATOMY, SHOWING
An Eye for a Dog. Robert Cole
Annie On Dogs! Ann Rogers Clark
Canine Cineradiography, DVD. Rachel Page Elliott
Canine Massage. Jean-Pierre Hourdebaigt
Canine Terminology (reprint). Harold Spira
Dog In Action (reprint). Macdowell Lyon
Dogsteps DVD. Rachel Page Elliott
Performance Dog Nutrition. Jocelynn Jacobs
Puppy Intensive Care. Myra Savant Harris
Raw Dog Food. Carina MacDonald
Raw Meaty Bones. Tom Lonsdale
Shock to the System. Catherine O'Driscoll
The History and Management of the Mastiff. Elizabeth Baxter & Pat Hoffman
Work Wonders. Tom Lonsdale
Whelping Healthy Puppies, DVD. Sylvia Smart

Dogwise.com is your complete source for dog books on the web!

2,000+ titles, fast shipping, and excellent customer service.